10 ⁰⁰

COLOUR
PROOF
CORRECTION
QUESTION
AND
ANSWER
BOOK

% Balance Kreuzmiren C 50%

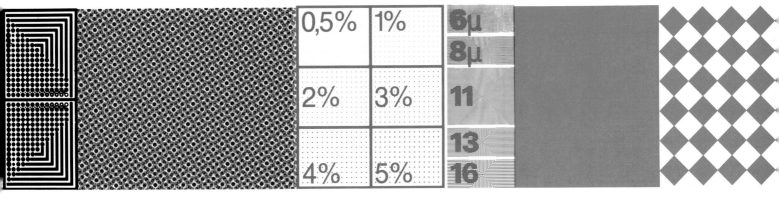

% 50% Balance Kreuzmiren C

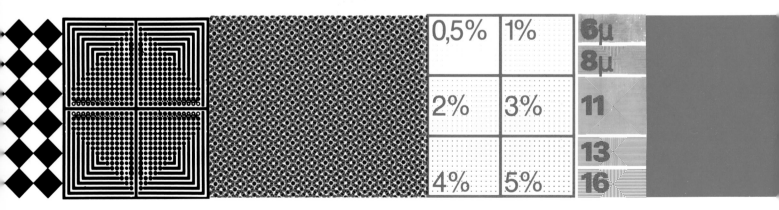

0,5%	1%
2%	3%
4%	5%

6μ
8μ
11
13
16

COLOUR

PROOF

CORRECTION

QUESTION

AND

ANSWER

BOOK

DAVID BANN & JOHN GARGAN

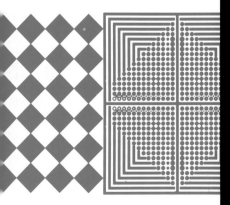

50% 50% M 50

PHAIDON · OXFORD

A QUARTO BOOK

Published by
Phaidon Press Limited
Musterlin House
Jordan Hill Road
Oxford OX2 8DP

First published 1990
Copyright © 1990
Quarto Publishing plc

A CIP catalogue record for this book is
available from the British Library

ISBN 0 7148 2663 4

This book was designed and produced
by Quarto Publishing plc,
The Old Brewery, 6 Blundell Street,
London N7 9BH

Typeset by Ampersand
Typesetting Limited, Bournemouth
Manufactured in Hong Kong by
Regent Publishing Services Limited
Printed in Singapore by
Tien Wah Press (Pte) Limited.

Consultants Duncan Ross,
Tony Farquharson

Senior Editor Kate Kirby
Editor Richard Dawes

Design Nick Clark
Picture Research Arlene Bridgewater
Illustrator David Kemp
Photographers Martin Norris,
Ian Howes, Paul Forrester

Art Director Moira Clinch
Assistant Art Director
Chloë Alexander

Special thanks go to
Grey Matter Design Consultants

The images in this book have been
proofed to the highest possible
standards. However, it should be
remembered that colour correction is
a subjective area open to individual
interpretation.
The colour bars reproduced in this
book are for use as a guide only. They
cannot be used for checking against
colour proofs.
This book contains examples of
graphic design work. These examples
are included for the purpose of
criticism and review.

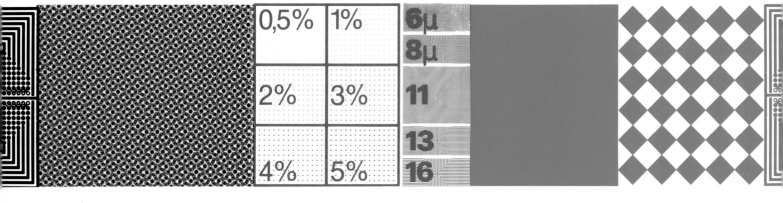

CONTENTS

SECTION ONE
All about proofs

This section explains what the four-colour process can achieve. The different methods of proofing are shown, as well as how the repro house produces final film and carries out corrections.

SECTION TWO
How to check colour proofs

This section explains in detail what the designer should look for when checking proofs; the equipment required; how to mark up proofs; and what colour bars are used for.

Examples are shown of proofs which are up or down in each of the four process colours or incorrect in other ways. Different subjects can present very different reproduction problems and a range is given, showing what can go wrong and how to correct it.

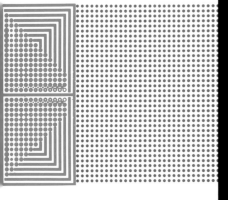

0% 25%

This linen tester is used throughout the book to show enlargements of particular details. The enlargement is usually 300%.

Use your own linen tester to look at other areas of the subjects and to familiarize yourself with which characteristics are important in achieving the final printed result.

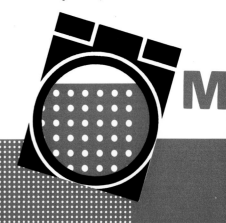

M

When reproducing a piece of work for printing, the client, the designer and the repro house may not have the same priorities. The client will want the job to look as good as possible, come in at the budgeted price and be delivered on time. The designer will also want the job to look as good as possible, but this priority may overshadow those of cost and schedule. The repro house has to translate the designer's concept into something which can be printed, and wants to make a profit and retain the client.

When things go wrong, it is nearly always due to poor communication between the three parties. This book is an attempt to improve communication by helping the designer to present artwork and layouts in the best way for the repro house and to mark up proofs so as to get the best possible results.

The designer's work does not stop at the layout stage; input is needed up to and during reproduction, proofing and printing. A good design will not succeed unless it can be translated effectively into the final printed job. I hope this book will help designers and repro houses to work as partners rather than, as sometimes happens, as adversaries.

David Bann
May 1990

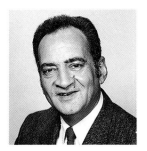

DAVID BANN is a graduate of the London College of Printing and a member of the Institute of Printing. He works on the production side of book publishing and is a director of Landmark Production Consultants. He has lectured extensively on book production and is the author of the *Print Production Handbook*.

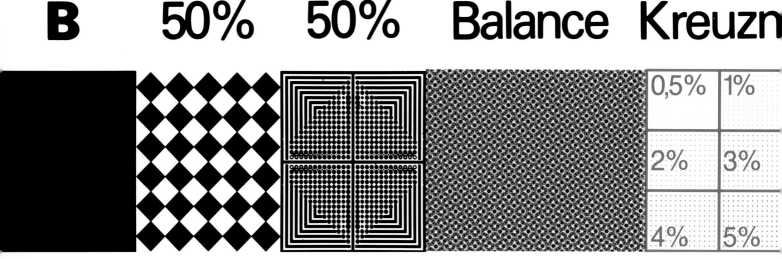

B 50% 50% Balance Kreuzn

0,5% 1%
2% 3%
4% 5%

I have been in repro longer than I care to remember, and in that time the industry has improved immensely. Better technology means that work can be reproduced more quickly, more efficiently and to a higher standard.

Today's designers are rightly more demanding and the industry has kept pace with their expectations. Also, there is now a better understanding between designers and repro houses. If it is the designer's vision which makes a printed job, it is the repro house's skills which help to realize that vision in the finished work.

Most of the content of this book is not taught in graphic design courses, and until now the designer has had to learn through first-hand experience. Here, David and I have tried to offer a short-cut to this knowledge. We have tried not to blind you with science but simply to give you the basic facts about proof correction and how to get the best from your repro house.

When a repro house has done a good job, it is always a pleasure to be told so, but we can also accept criticism when it is justified. As an industry, we do listen.

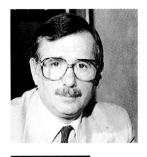

JOHN GARGAN has thirty years' experience in colour reproduction. He started his career as a colour planner and now runs Colour Solutions, a reproduction house and part of Omnicom, one of the largest communication companies in the world.

John Gargan
May 1990

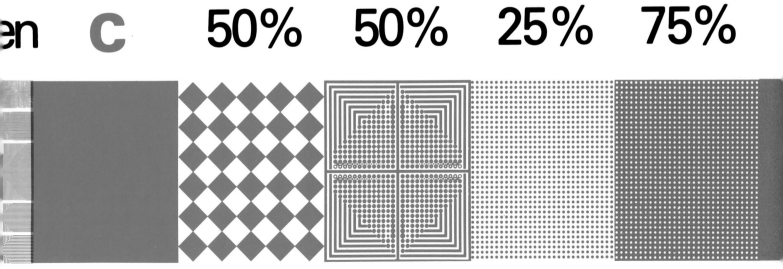

en   C   50%   50%   25%   75%

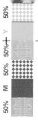

Sending material to the repro house

THREE CRITERIA govern the selection of a supplier – price, quality and service. Each of these aspects is discussed below.

PRICE In colour separation, prices can vary a lot from one supplier to another, depending on location, equipment and type of work undertaken.

Colour separation suppliers can be found in large cities and country areas across the UK, as well as in Europe and the Far East. The schedule will determine whether the work can be placed abroad or even outside the town or city where the client and designer are located. Courier services enable packages to be in other parts of the UK or Europe the next day and in the Far East in a maximum of 48 hours. However, the timing of many jobs is so critical that work must be dealt with the same day, which restricts the choice to local repro houses.

In practice, reproduction is only done abroad on large jobs such as books or catalogues where there is an extended schedule. A typical repro house in Singapore or Hong Kong will reproduce and proof 200 transparencies in 14 days including transit time, and at a cost considerably lower than UK prices. However, this is the first proof stage and after this time must be allowed

for checking and returning the proofs and seeing reproofs of some subjects before the production of final film. Checking and correction can extend the total time for a large job to three to four weeks. Another factor is that repro houses outside large cities are usually cheaper because of lower rates of pay. Price is also related to service, and while repro houses which work round the clock have to pay (and charge) more for shift work, they can often turn jobs round overnight.

QUALITY The quality offered by a repro house depends on the equipment it has, as well as on the ability of the staff and their experience in dealing with the type of work in hand. Some repro houses specialize in book work, some in packaging and some in magazines or corporate work such as company annual reports.

To establish a repro house's quality, you can ask to see samples, visit the factory or get the recommendation of other customers. The last option is probably the best guide, for if someone whose opinion you respect has used a repro house over a period of time and can recommend it, then that repro house should be considered. The printer you are using for the job will have experience of different repro houses and should also be in a position to recommend several.

SERVICE A repro house which provides good service will meet all the proof dates and the date for final film and, if possible, will make up time if jobs run late at any stage. Good service also means

WHAT TO ASK A REPRO HOUSE BEFORE COMMISSIONING A JOB

1 How long until first proofs?
2 On approval, how long until final film?
3 Have you done work of this nature and can you show me samples?
4 Who are your main customers?
5 What equipment do you have?
6 Do you work 24 hours a day?
7 Have you won any awards for your work?
8 Do you collect and deliver?

responding quickly to queries and paying close attention to detail. Service is obviously of vital importance on dated items such as magazines.

SPECIFICATION When you have shortlisted three or four repro houses which can meet the price, quality and service criteria, the next step is to draw up a specification for the job (see opposite).

The specification for reproduction should indicate the number of originals, whether they are transparencies or flat artworks, the size at which they are to appear, whether or not any of the originals are "in pro" (in proportion – that is, to the same percentage reduction or enlargement; see pages 40-41), the page size, whether pictures bleed, whether proofs are to be scatter or page proofs and the number and type of proofs required, e.g. Cromalins or wet proofs (see pages 56-57).

Black and white pictures should be described as halftone or line. The final product required should be stated (e.g. scanned sets or final positives and whether random or paged). Where wet proofs are being produced, the repro house should always be asked to supply progressives (see pages 58-59) to the printer. With wet proofing, the specification should include the type of paper required.

Always state how long the prices should be valid, as repro houses have periodic increases because of pay increases or inflation. If you can send a copy of the layout, this will greatly help the repro house to prepare an accurate estimate.

THE ESTIMATE When you receive the repro house's estimate, check carefully that it accords with the specification. Most repro houses use the phrase "subject to sight of artwork" on their estimate, in case any subjects need special treatment. If possible, include any such requirements in the specification.

If the prospective suppliers all offer the same standard of quality and service, then normally the one quoting the lowest price will get the work. However, prices are usually negotiable and if you are keen to give the work to a particular repro house, you may be able to negotiate the price down to match that offered by a competitor.

When the designer requotes the selected supplier's price to the client, it is wise to add a contingency of 10% or more to allow for unforeseen problems.

EXTRAS Once the job is in hand, extra costs ("extras") may arise for a number of reasons. It is important, where any major extra work is required, that the repro house advise you before carrying it out, so that you can inform the client and avoid a three-way argument at invoice stage. A common area of contention is reproofing. In cases where the original proof was not up to standard, the repro house should not charge the cost of reproofing. However, it is justified in charging if the designer changes the size or asks for a different colour result than in the original.

A brochure   From: A customer   To: A repro house

Please quote for reproduction and proofing to the following specification:

Trimmed Page Size: 297 × 210mm, full bleeds   Extent: 32 pages self-cover

8 black and white halftones (× half-page) out of pro
10 black and white line illustrations (× quarter-page) in pro
20 transparencies out of pro – sizes as follows:
8 × full-page
6 × half-page
6 × quarter-page
Rules and tint-laying as attached layout
Type supplied as camera-ready copy in page form

Please supply 12 sets of page proofs in double-page spreads on 135gsm matt-coated cartridge paper. On approval, supply final film positives, right-reading emulsion-down, in page form and progressives.
Make prices valid to December 1990.

SPEC SHEET FOR A REPRO HOUSE

Originals for reproduction

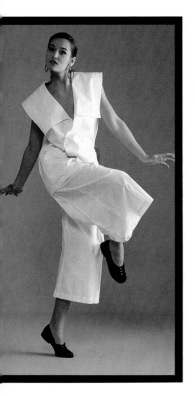

Transcription Transparencies should always be protected by a plastic sleeve.

Glass mounts should be removed as they may break in transit and damage the original. Flat artwork should be covered to protect the surface.

Never use paper-clips on halftone originals as the scanner picks up the impression and it can appear on the proof.

THE REPRO HOUSE needs good originals to do a good job and the careful selection and preparation of these is a vital component of a successful result.

LINE ORIGINALS Unlike most photographs for reproduction, line originals are often specially commissioned, which means that when briefing the artist you can ensure that they are prepared in the most suitable way for reproduction.

A line original should be black and may be drawn larger than the size at which it is to appear, in which case any slight inaccuracies in the artwork will be minimized when it is reduced. It should be mounted on stable board and should include trim and bleed marks. Tints can be laid by the artist, but tints laid by the repro house are usually cleaner, though slightly more expensive.

Any alterations or corrections to drawings should be free of blemishes. Watch for this particularly where the artist has made a correction.

You can give the size either as a linear measurement (e.g. reduce width to 110mm) or as a percentage reduction or enlargement (e.g. reduce to 66% of original size). Same-size reproduction is indicated by "S/S". The required crop can be shown by a traced overlay or a photocopy to the correct dimensions.

TYPE Typeset material is treated like a line original by the reproduction process. CRC (camera-ready copy) should be mounted on a base firm enough to prevent any stuck-down copy becoming detached if the base is flexed. CS10 board is a suitable base for most jobs. Where type is set as complete pages

of bromide with nothing stuck down, it does not require a base.

Grids should be printed in pale, non-reproducing blue and the same colour should be used by the designer for any written instructions on the CRC. (The camera will pick up any other colour and the repro house will have to touch it out on the film.)

It is important that the setting itself has been correctly exposed and developed, to give a sharp image of consistent density. Where correction lines have been stripped in, ensure that they are the same density as the initial setting. If there is a correction to just one line, it is better to reset a "patch" of three or four lines as this will avoid or at least reduce any density variation.

Where type is reversed out of colour or overprints a colour, particular care must be taken (see pages 132–133).

COLOUR PHOTOGRAPHS These can either be transparencies or prints, the former giving a brighter, sharper result. The original should have reasonable contrast and there should be no overall colour cast. (However, if there is a colour cast and no alternative original is available, then the repro house can be alerted to it and will probably be able to lose it in scanning – see page 37.) Images with excessive grain should be avoided as this will show up, particularly if the picture is enlarged. A big enlargement can cause problems, especially when it is from a 35mm original (see pages 40–41).

Original transparencies should be used where possible as duplicating a transparency increases density. The sizing of transparencies is done in the same way as for black and white line and halftone work.

In the absence of any instructions, the repro house will attempt to match the transparency, so if the designer requires something to be altered (such as losing a colour cast or making a transparency brighter), it is important to mention it when the job is begun, rather than at proof stage.

Where colour is important, as in photographs of works of art, the photographer will include a colour scale in the transparency outside the area to be used. This scale is called a colour-control patch and indicates any colour bias there may be in the transparency. This bias may be caused by a mismatch between the lighting conditions and the film or may be due to the natural fading of a transparency, which tends to occur over a period of time. These patches are useful both in the processing of film and to alert the repro house to any colour cast.

BLACK AND WHITE HALFTONES Photographs to be reproduced as halftones should have good contrast and detail (see pages 82-83) and be free from blemishes. Photographs can be retouched to remove blemishes, or to improve contrast or detail. However, this is expensive and where scanners are used, sometimes the retouching marks will show up on the final result. Any retouching should be discussed with the repro house before reproduction.

Black and white halftone originals can be reproduced in four colour to give more depth and detail, although this is more expensive (see pages 86-87).

Sizing and cropping are done as for line.

COLOUR FLAT ARTWORK The presentation of colour flat artwork is described in detail on page 42. Very large originals may be too big to fit round the drum of the scanner and the designer may need to have a transparency made.

SPECIAL COLOURS AND TINTS These can present particular problems (see pages 44-45).

IDENTIFYING ORIGINALS All originals should carry a figure number and page number (if known). The repro house can then be asked to put these numbers on the film and proofs of each subject, to assist the identification of subjects. This is particularly important on large jobs which are scatter-proofed.

INSURANCE Many transparencies are valued by the photographer at around £400 ($660) and some at as much as £2,000 ($3,300). It is normally the client's responsibility to insure originals against loss or damage occurring either at the design studio or the repro house, or in transit. It is worth checking the insurance cover with both the client and the repro house. If a repro house loses or damages an original, it will normally offer some compensation, but not necessarily to the same value as that put on it by the photographer or artist.

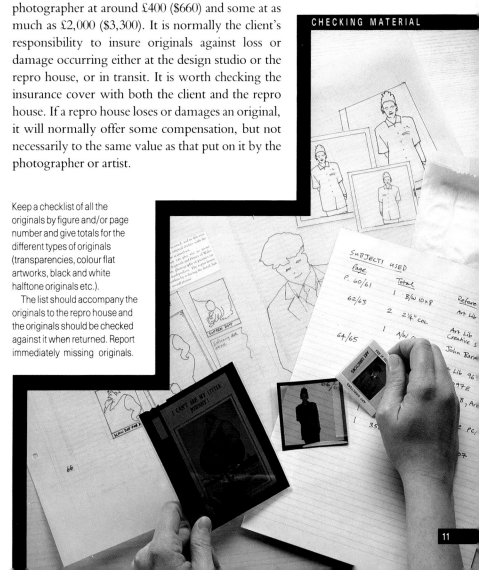

CHECKING MATERIAL

Keep a checklist of all the originals by figure and/or page number and give totals for the different types of originals (transparencies, colour flat artworks, black and white halftone originals etc.).

The list should accompany the originals to the repro house and the originals should be checked against it when returned. Report immediately missing originals.

Reproduction techniques
Lithography and other processes

EFFECTIVE CORRECTION of colour proofs demands at least a basic knowledge of reproduction techniques, in order that the designer can understand the possibilities and limitations of the reproduction and printing process.

Offset lithography is the process used for the majority of work handled by designers and this section deals with reproduction by this process.

LINE ORIGINATION The original, which is normally black and white, is placed on the copy board of a process camera. The process camera is a very large version of an ordinary camera and works in a similar way to the PMT (photomechanical transfer) machines used by designers. Film coated with a light-sensitive emulsion is placed in the back of the camera, behind the lens. The original is lit with a bright light and the shutter of the camera opened to expose the image onto the film.

On exposure, light reflected from the white area of the original passes through the lens to fall on the film emulsion, which contains silver halide that responds to light and blackens during development. When the film has been developed to produce a negative, unexposed silver, which will not have blackened, is dissolved in a fixing solution. The negative can be used for platemaking or contact printed to make a positive in cases where plates need positives rather than negatives, normally for colour work.

The size of the image is determined by adjusting the lens and the copy board on the camera and the exposure is timed to ensure that the film image is neither underexposed ("thick") nor overexposed ("thin").

Typeset material is treated as a line original when supplied in the form of CRC and is shot on a camera in the same way. In some cases the filmsetting machine can produce a negative or positive and this makes it unnecessary for the type to be shot.

HALFTONE ORIGINATION A continuous-tone original, such as a black and white photograph, cannot be shot as line, as the different shades of grey will not be picked up by the camera. This type of original has to be reproduced as a halftone.

The different shades of grey in a black and white photograph cannot be printed in grey, as in this case

Nearly all colour separation is now done on scanners like this. Scanning has replaced separation on camera and is faster, cheaper and gives much more control. Scanners can be linked to other electronic equipment to produce complete made-up pages.

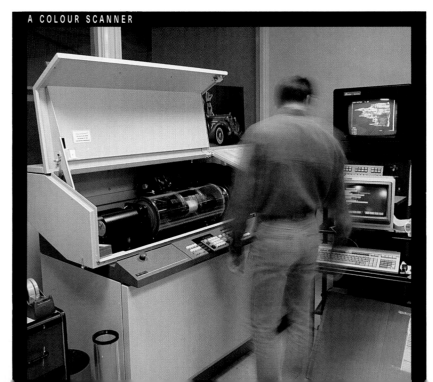

A COLOUR SCANNER

the printing press uses only black ink. The halftone process therefore simulates the greys by breaking the picture up into small dots. These are largest in the dark areas and smallest in the pale areas. When printed, this arrangement gives the effect of the different shades of grey, even though only black ink has been used.

Halftones can be reproduced on process cameras, although now most are scanned. In the case of camera reproduction, the halftone effect is achieved by placing a screen in the back of the camera between the lens and the film. The screen, made of film, has a grid of fine lines which breaks the image up into dots, producing a halftone negative. In black and white reproduction, the halftone screen is normally placed at an angle of 45° to the horizontal, as this makes the rows of dots less obvious to the eye.

Another camera technique used for halftones is to produce a continuous-tone negative on the process camera and place a contact screen between the negative and a sheet of unexposed film, which becomes a screened positive on exposure.

Screens can be coarse or fine and screen rulings are described in detail on pages 50-51.

Halftones can also be produced as PMTs. A PMT is a screened halftone print on photographic paper and designers with PMT machines can produce these in the studio. As the PMT is already screened, it can be pasted into CRC and the whole paste-up can then be photographed as a line shot. This saves the expense of shooting the photographs onto film and stripping them in at the film stage.

However, screened PMTs cannot give first-rate quality and should probably not be used finer than 120 screen. Therefore the designer must be discriminating in the type of job for which PMTs are used.

The majority of pencil drawings are treated as halftones in order to reproduce the subtle shades of

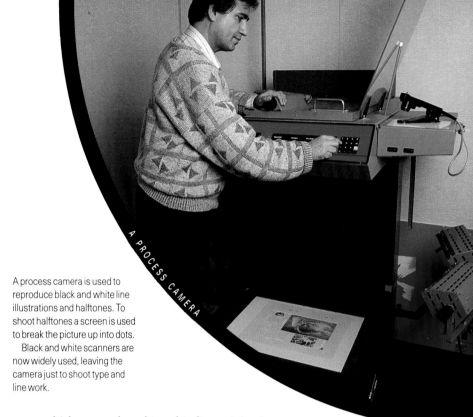

A process camera is used to reproduce black and white line illustrations and halftones. To shoot halftones a screen is used to break the picture up into dots.

Black and white scanners are now widely used, leaving the camera just to shoot type and line work.

grey, which cannot be achieved in line origination. The background can be dropped out so that it carries no dot pattern, but is just white paper.

SCANNING HALFTONES Until fairly recently, most halftones were reproduced on cameras, as scanners were available only for four-colour process work. However, a new generation of monochrome scanners has ensured that the majority of halftone work is now scanned. A scanner's end product is a screened positive, as with a camera, but as this is produced by electronic means there is much more control over the process resulting in much better quality. It is also cheaper and there is a higher throughput. The scanning of black and white halftones uses the same basic principles as scanning colour (see page 14).

The characteristics of good black and white halftone originals and reproductions are discussed on pages 82-83. Sometimes black and white photo-

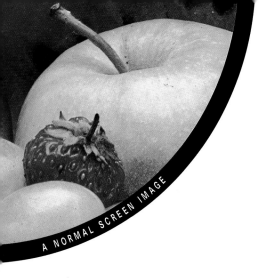

A NORMAL SCREEN IMAGE

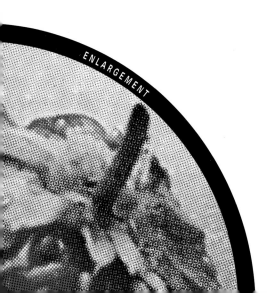

ENLARGEMENT

To separate colour originals the halftone principle is used in the same way as for black and white photographs. Each colour film is made up of dots of sizes that differ according to the density of colour in the corresponding area of the original. A normal 133-screen image (above) is shown enlarged 400% (below).

Dots of the four process colours enlarged are shown right.

To avoid screen clash, or moiré, the screen lines are set at different angles to each other.

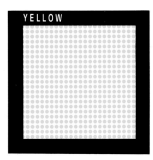

YELLOW

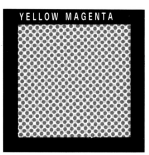

YELLOW MAGENTA

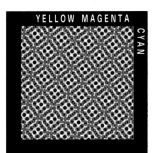

YELLOW MAGENTA CYAN

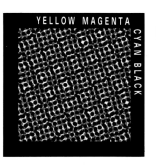

YELLOW MAGENTA CYAN BLACK

graphs are reproduced by the four-colour process to give more depth (see pages 86–87). These are scanned in exactly the same way as four-colour sets.

DUOTONES A duotone is a two-colour halftone (see pages 84–85). It can be produced on a camera or scanner as described above, but two negatives are produced rather than one.

LINE AND TONE A combination of line and halftone is a negative contacted from two films – one line and the other halftone. The process is used, for example, where solid type is to appear superimposed on a photograph.

COLOUR SEPARATION Colour originals must be "separated" so that the effect of full colour can be achieved by printing in only four colours. This is done by breaking down the original into three colours – magenta, cyan and yellow, to which black is added to give finer detail and add density to dark areas.

Known as the "four-colour process", this operation results in four pieces of film. It is possible to reproduce most colours from combinations of two or more of these four colours. For example, a purple is produced by putting a certain amount of magenta with a certain amount of cyan, the proportions varying according to the particular shade required.

However, certain colours are impossible to produce accurately with the four-colour process (see pages 44–45).

SCANNING Above is described the basic separation process as done on a camera, but nearly all separation is now carried out on scanners. The same separation principles apply, but the scanner uses a high-intensity light or laser beam to scan the original and separate the colours. The colour filters and a computer are built into the scanner and convert the signals picked up by the beam into screened posi-

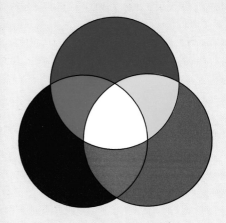

"White" light is a combination of all the colours of the spectrum. These can be broken down into three "primary" colours – red, green and blue. Since these three colours when added together make white light, they are known as the "additive" primaries (above). When one is taken away, the other two combined make a different colour. Red and blue produce magenta, while green and blue give cyan. Magenta, cyan and yellow are "subtractive" primaries or "secondary" colours (below).

In printing, the four process colours are the three subtractive primaries – magenta, cyan and yellow – and black. To make a film that will produce the required colour, a filter is used of the respective additive primary colour (right). For example, to make a negative film for the yellow, a blue filter is used. This absorbs all the wavelengths of light reflected from the yellow components of the original, so that yellow is not recorded on the emulsion. When developed, the "black" part of the negative will represent everything in the original which is not yellow and the clear part therefore includes all the yellow components of the original. Similarly, a green filter will produce a negative for the magenta and a red filter a negative for the cyan.

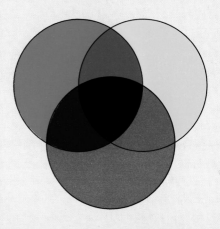

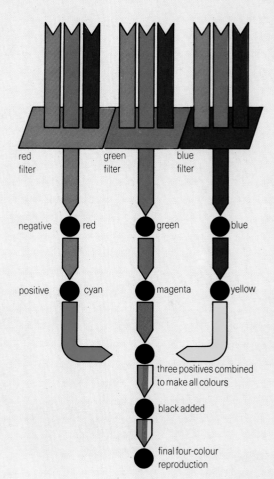

red filter   green filter   blue filter

negative   red   green   blue

positive   cyan   magenta   yellow

three positives combined to make all colours

black added

final four-colour reproduction

tives for each of the four colours.

Compared with a process camera, the scanner is much faster and gives superior quality, and most modern scanners can separate all four colours at once. The scanner operator has access to a range of sophisticated electronic controls which can achieve a faithfulness to the original that, with camera separation, could be achieved only by retouching the separated film.

If a job has originals that are to be reduced or enlarged by the same percentage, these can be scanned together, saving cost. These originals are described as "in pro" (in proportion). However, in addition to the same reduction or enlargement, the originals must also have similar density ranges, otherwise the scanner settings which suit one original will not give a good result with another. In such cases it can be left to the repro house to decide what to do.

The originals are taped to the drum of the scanner and the scanner operator sets the percentage enlargement or reduction and the screen ruling. A densitometer is used to take readings of the density of colours in different parts of the original and then the scanner is set up accordingly.

The scanner drum holding the original rotates at high speed and the scanning head analyses the image as it moves along the drum. The signals are sent via the colour filters to the computer, which converts the digital information into light signals that are exposed on film.

Colour flat artwork is scanned in the same way, but must be on flexible board so that it can be wrapped around the drum. Colour artwork can contain strong hues which are difficult to reproduce in four colours.

Most modern scanners use a laser beam and produce a hard dot (see page 60) which limits the amount of hand retouching.

While most scanners use rotating drums for inputting scanned images, some now use a flat bed system. Usually these are mono scanners – that is, only for black and white. However, some repro houses do offer a flat bed system which will take colour transparencies or flat artwork, though no bigger than 20 × 25cm (8 × 10in).

The best-known manufacturers of scanners are Crosfield, Hell, Dai Nippon and Itek. Each makes several different models with different features and capable of taking a variety of sizes of originals.

ELECTRONIC PAGE MAKE-UP Now in common use, electronic page make-up systems can scan, store

For small-scale scanning the transparency is fixed to the drum with either an adhesive lacquer (below) or tape (inset).

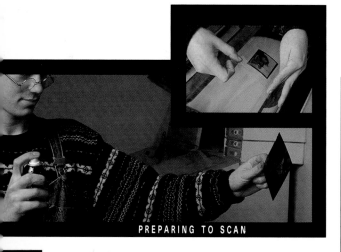

PREPARING TO SCAN

MAKING BIG ENLARGEMENTS

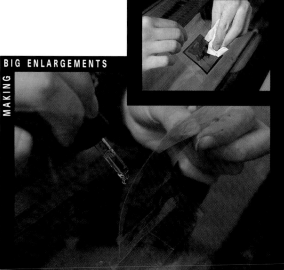

When a big enlargement is required, the surface is covered with oil to minimize the effects of surface scratches (left). The oil is held in place by clear plastic foil (inset).

the separation information on a hard disk in digital form, and then use it to create complete pages with several transparencies, tints and rules. The resulting page films are one-piece films for each colour. In addition, electronic page make-up systems can produce shapes and cut-outs, do airbrushing and vignetting and carry out colour correction.

Most of these systems have a colour monitor, enabling the operator to check everything before it is committed to film. Some systems can include type as well as pictures in the layout and can even alter typefaces and type sizes at layout stage.

These systems are very costly, but their sophistication enables repro houses to produce complex publications such as mail order catalogues more economically and with better results. As well as these complete systems, there are also independent work stations which can interface with the scanner.

Nearly all these systems are installed in repro houses rather than design studios. However, designers in some larger magazine companies are now turning to electronic page make-up. The advantage is that the design is done in "real time". This means that when the designer changes the size of an image the operation is carried out there and then, rather than a design decision being enacted by the repro house at a later stage.

DESKTOP PUBLISHING Until recently, desktop publishing (DTP) has been used mainly for typesetting work with line illustration and simple black and white halftones. However, there is now a blurring of the distinction between DTP and electronic page make-up. DTP allows the designer to design a page of typesetting, pictures in black and white and colour, as well as tints/rules etc. and end up with a disk containing all this information, which can be sent to the repro house for outputting onto film.

CAD DRAFTING AND MASKING SYSTEMS Computer systems perform some of the functions of electronic page make-up systems, such as tint laying, drafting and masking, but are much cheaper than the full systems.

TINTS Where the designer requires a flat area of colour, the repro house normally produces it by using tints. A tint is not solid ink, but is made up from dots of the four process colours. The colours are screened in percentages, usually in increments of 10%, and a tint may consist of one process colour or be combined with one or more of the other three colours. This yields a possible 1,400 combinations.

When a special colour is to be matched by using the four-colour process, it is always better to specify

After scanning, the film is developed and fixed in a film processor (below). The final piece of film for one of the four process colours (inset).

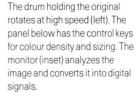

The drum holding the original rotates at high speed (left). The panel below has the control keys for colour density and sizing. The monitor (inset) analyzes the image and converts it into digital signals.

SCANNING

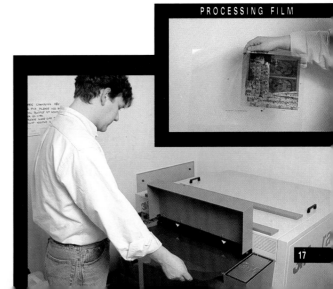

PROCESSING FILM

17

the percentages of different colours as above, rather than give a colour swatch or PANTONE®★ reference and ask the repro house to match it. Some special colours cannot be exactly matched from the process and rather than find this out at proof stage, it is better to specify a tint knowing that the repro house will be able to match it (see pages 44-45).

DOT GAIN Describes the increase in size of the dot from film dot to printed dot (see pages 62-63).

UNDERCOLOUR REMOVAL This and achromatic reproduction are explained on pages 46-47.

PROOFING Once film has been made, a proof is produced so that the client, designer and repro house can check the quality, sizing and positioning. The printer will also require a proof to match when printing the job.

Where jobs are varnished, laminated or foil blocked, or have some other kind of special finish, the repro house can usually send the proofs to the finishing supplier to have the operation carried out, so that the proof has all the characteristics of the finished job. However, these finishing operations can usually only be carried out on wet proofs on paper, as the photographic material used in Cromalins and Matchprints cannot be laminated, varnished or foil blocked. Note also that in order to block, a mould will have to be made and artwork supplied for this at the same time as the other originals.

CHECKING COLOUR PROOFS The checking of colour proofs is dealt with in detail on page 80.

PASSING COLOUR ON MACHINE The question on page 141 describes how to check colour at the printing stage.

FILM ASSEMBLY This term describes the assembly of all the type and pictorial elements within a page in the correct position. In most cases, the typesetter or designer will already have positioned the type in page form as camera-ready copy, leaving spaces for any illustrations. The repro house will shoot the CRC (see page 12) and make negative or positive film from it.

If the repro house is to produce scatter proofs (see pages 56-57) and random film, the assembly will be done by the printer at the same time as imposition.

IMPOSITION This is the placing of the pages in the correct position on the plate so that in the finished job they come out in the right order and with the correct margins.

A typical electronic page make-up system consists of a colour monitor, a keyboard and a "mouse". The operator manipulates the images and type to fit the designer's layout (below).

When checked, page film is produced on the output scanner. This avoids all the handwork involved in combining the different elements using conventional reproduction techniques.

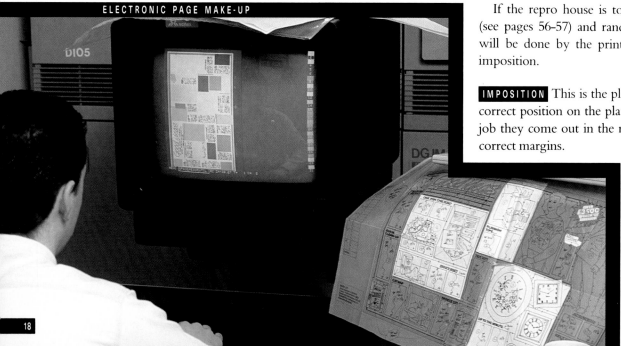

ELECTRONIC PAGE MAKE-UP

*Pantone, Inc's check standard trademark for colour reproduction and colour reproduction materials.

Most presses print 8, 16 or 32 pages (or multiples of these) to view (on one side of the paper) and the printer works out an imposition scheme that will print the required number of pages in the most economical way on the press being used. The designer will not normally need to know the details of the imposition unless part of the job is being printed in a different number of colours (e.g. four colours backing two). Here the designer will need to get the imposition scheme from the printer, to establish which pages are printed in the different ways. The illustrations and layout can then be planned according to which pages are printed in four colours and which in two.

The imposition itself is normally done with adhesive tape on clear plastic foils, which are positioned on top of the layout grid. This is a slow and expensive hand operation and some printers now use electronic imposition systems, such as Opticopy or Rachwal.

The Opticopy is basically a camera which holds a very large piece of film the same size as the printing plate. The pages are photographed one at a time and the machine moves the film each time, exposing each page in the correct position for printing. The operation is controlled by a computer with different programmes for the required imposition schemes.

The Rachwal system photographs each page onto a reel of 70mm film. This is then put into a projection head which enlarges the page to full size and exposes it directly onto the printing plate.

Another machine which automates imposition is the "step and repeat" machine. This has a projection head containing negative or positive film, which is moved automatically under computer control and exposes the image onto the plate each time it moves. This machine is used particularly for making plates which have multiple copies of the same image. For example, it is used a lot in packaging, where a small carton might be printed with 32 or more of the same image on the plate.

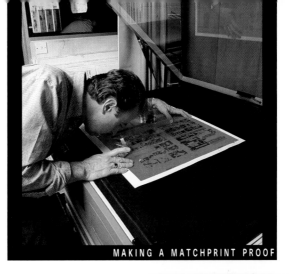

MAKING A MATCHPRINT PROOF

The magenta film is being placed over the red laminate before exposure (left). The process is repeated for the other three colours.

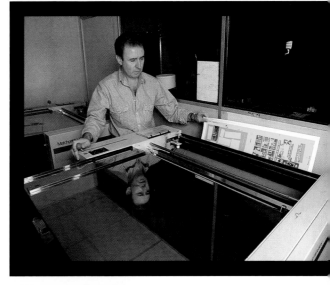

The yellow laminate being applied to the base sheet after the cyan and magenta have been processed (right).

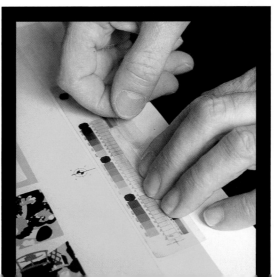

The colour bar for the yellow is being placed in contact with the yellow laminate (left). The colour bar will show not only the density of colour being used, but also dot gain and other characteristics of the proof.

OZALIDS After imposition, the printer makes ozalids from the imposed foils. Ozalids are produced by a process similar to that used for dye-line prints: the imposed foil is placed over the ozalid paper which is photosensitized. The paper is then exposed to light and the ozalid developed to give a proof in either black or blue on white, or sometimes a "negative" in which the image is in white on black or blue. It is possible to produce two-sided ozalids, rule them up and fold them, so that the designer can see exactly how the job will print.

PLATEMAKING When the ozalids have been approved, the printer corrects the foils as necessary and then makes printing plates from the imposed foils.

REPRODUCTION FOR OTHER PROCESSES:
LETTERPRESS In the letterpress process (see pages 24–25), pictures are printed from letterpress "blocks"; that is, plates which have a raised surface for the image area. The first part of the reproduction process is the same as for offset lithography. The original is placed on a camera and a line or halftone negative is made exactly as described for offset printing.

Blocks are very expensive compared with offset plates and this is one of the reasons why the letterpress process has been supplanted by offset lithography except for certain specialized types of work.

Origination for screen printing In screen printing (see pages 27–28), the image is produced by the use of a stencil which can be made either by hand or photographically.

Hand-cut stencils are made using film with two layers. The stencil is cut on the top layer, following a layout, and those areas where the image is to appear are cut out with a sharp knife, leaving the backing film behind. The film is transferred to the screen and the backing film peeled away to leave the film blocking the openings of the mesh in the non-printing areas.

Normally jobs are imposed as sheet work (below left) in which half the pages in the job are on each side of the sheet.

Some jobs are imposed for half-sheet work (below right) which is also known as "work and turn". This means that all the pages in a job are printed on one side of the sheet and the sheet is then turned over and the other side printed on. In this way each sheet produces two copies of the job.

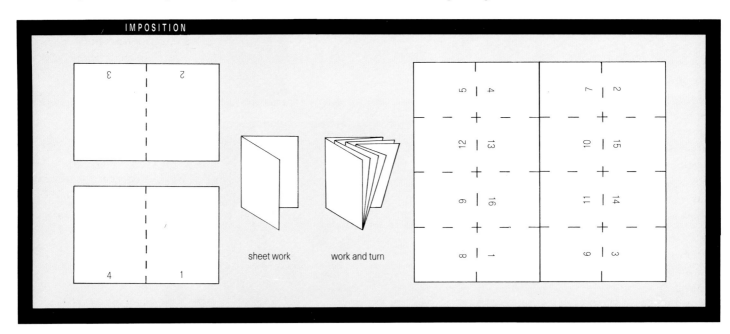

IMPOSITION

sheet work   work and turn

It is not practical to use hand-cut stencils for small type, photographs or fine drawings and so a photographic process is used for this type of work. Photostencils can be produced either by the indirect or direct method. In the indirect method, a positive is produced (using halftone and four-colour processes as for offset lithography) and this is placed in contact with the stencil film and exposed to light. The image areas are hardened and the non-image areas on the coating are soft and can be washed away with chemicals. The stencil is then transferred to the screen and the backing film removed. This leaves the mesh blocked by the light-hardened areas of coating on the non-image areas.

In the direct method, light-sensitive solution is applied directly to the screen and after exposure the soft (image) areas of the coating are washed away with chemicals.

Origination for gravure The image in gravure is recessed into a plate or cylinder. The gravure cylinder is made of solid steel electroplated with a thin, highly polished copper skin which forms the printing surface. Gravure cylinders are often chromium-plated to prevent wear on long runs. For sheet-fed gravure, a thin copper plate is wrapped round the plate cylinder of the press.

Before modern electronic methods of preparing gravure cylinders, the reproduction process started with continuous-tone (unscreened) positives for each colour of the four-colour process. Type is shot to make a line negative which is exposed to combine with the continous-tone positive of the pictures. This film is then contacted to a gelatin transfer medium called "carbon tissue", previously screened by exposing it to light in contact with a 150-line glass screen.

This screen consists of small opaque squares surrounded by transparent lines. These lines create the walls of the cells which hold the ink.

The screened carbon tissue is then exposed to the positive carrying the image. The next stage is to lay the carbon tissue around the cylinder and develop it to wash away any unhardened gelatin, leaving gelatin of varying thickness on the cylinder. The cylinder is then etched with ferric chloride, the rate of penetration depending on the thickness of the gelatin. This results in cells of differing depths, the deepest ones being for the dark areas of the subject and carrying the most ink, while the shallower cells correspond to the lighter areas of the subject.

The above technique has now been almost completely replaced by "litho-to-gravure" conversion using the halftone technique. Here, scanning is carried out exactly as for offset litho origination, except that the scanner is set up slightly differently to allow for the fact that the minimum highlight dot in gravure is 5% compared with 2–3% for litho.

The screened positives (150 screen) are then planned as for litho, with the type in position, and this planned foil is contacted to a white plastic material called "opaline". There is a sheet of opaline for each of the four colours and it consists of screened images of one of the four colours, with the type being on the black opaline.

A laser cylinder gravure engraving machine (such as a Klischograph) is used to engrave the cylinder. A scanning head reads the opaline and transmits signals to a laser beam which cuts out the cells (earlier machines have a diamond engraving head).

The gravure process also uses electronic page make-up systems in which the complete pages are made up electronically as for litho. The system produces complete page positives from which the opalines are made. More advanced systems cut out film and opaline together and engrave the cylinder directly.

Electronic engraving is cheaper and more accurate than the previously used chemical methods and is helping to bring down gravure origination costs and so enable the process to compete on shorter runs than previously.

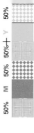

Printing processes
Offset lithography • Letterpress • Gravure • Screen printing • Foil blocking • Embossing

THE MAIN PRINTING PROCESS used now is offset lithography, on which this chapter will concentrate. However, from time to time designers will deal with work produced by the other processes, such as letterpress, flexography, gravure or screen printing.

The printing surfaces used by letterpress, lithography and gravure have different physical characteristics. Letterpress is a "relief" process in which the image to be printed is raised above the background. This raised surface is inked by rollers and then pressed against the paper to make the impression. Lithography is "planographic"; that is, using a flat printing surface. The image area is chemically treated so that it accepts ink and rejects water, while the non-image area is treated to accept

water and reject ink. Gravure is an "intaglio" process, in which the printing image is recessed into the plate and filled with liquid ink. The non-image area is wiped free of ink, so the ink is deposited on the paper from the recessed cells only.

OFFSET LITHOGRAPHY This is the predominant printing process being used for a wide range of items from stationery to books and magazines. Lithography was invented by Aloïs Senefelder in Bavaria in 1798, but it was only when the offset principle was applied early in the present century that lithography started to be used for commercial (as opposed to art) printing. It was as recently as the 1960s that the offset lithography process began gradually to overtake

THE LITHOGRAPHY PROCESS

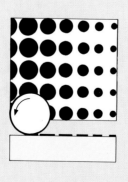

Lithography has a planographic (flat) printing surface. The image area accepts ink and repels water. The non-image area repels ink and attracts water. The four diagrams on the right show the original lithographic process, which printed directly onto paper. Nearly all lithographic printing is now done by offset lithography (or "offset"), which is shown on the opposite page.

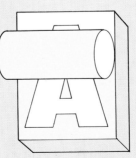

The image area of the plate is first treated with a greasy medium and then dampened with water by rollers.

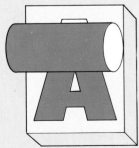

The plate is inked by rollers, the ink adhering to the greasy image but not to the dampened areas.

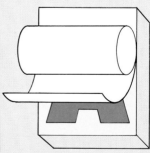

The paper is pressed against the plate.

letterpress as the main printing process.

In lithography (litho) the printing surface is flat rather than raised, as in letterpress, or recessed, as in gravure. The area to be printed is treated chemically so that it accepts grease (ink) and rejects water, while the non-image (background) area is treated to accept water and reject grease (ink). The surface of the printing plate has both water and ink applied to it. When the inked and dampened plate is pressed against the paper, only the image area is printed.

Lithographic printing was first done using smooth stone slabs as the printing surface and this method is still used by artists to make original lithographic prints. Modern offset lithography uses plates made of grained aluminium.

The offset press The offset press carries out the operations of feeding, damping (applying water to the plate), inking, printing and delivering the finished sheet.

The rotary principle is used in which the press acts rather as a mangle, with the cylinders rolling against each other. The printing section of the press consists of three cylinders – a blanket cylinder around which a sheet of rubber is wrapped, a plate cylinder carrying the printing plate, and the impression cylinder which presses the paper against the blanket to make the impression.

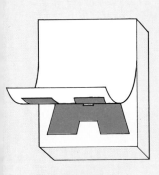

The final printed image.

In offset printing the inked image on the metal plate is offset (printed) onto a rubber blanket wrapped round a rotating metal cylinder and the image is then transferred from the blanket to the paper. The reason for printing via the blanket rather than directly from plate onto paper is that the plate's surface is delicate.

If the plate came into contact with the abrasive paper surface, rapid wear on the plate would occur.

Another advantage of the offset principle is that less water comes

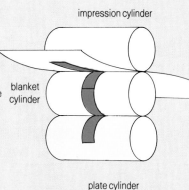

impression cylinder

blanket cylinder

plate cylinder

into contact with the paper, so avoiding problems of paper shrinkage which would give rise to register (positioning) problems. Also, being slightly elastic, the rubber blanket responds to surface irregularities, so that it is possible to print on a wide variety of surfaces.

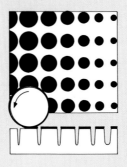

Letterpress is a "relief" process – that is, the printing surface holding the image to be printed is raised above the non-printing background. The raised surface is inked by rollers and then pressed against the paper to make the impression. The background does not print because, being lower than the printing area, it does not come into contact with either the inking rollers or the paper.

In traditional letterpress, all the text is printed from metal type and the pictures from letterpress blocks. These elements are assembled together (imposed) to make a "forme" inside a rigid frame or "chase", which is placed in the press. The printing surface is therefore made up of hundreds or thousands of different pieces of type, blocks and spacing (left).

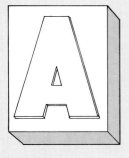
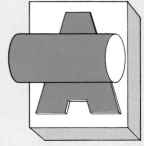
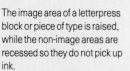

The image area of a letterpress block or piece of type is raised, while the non-image areas are recessed so they do not pick up ink.

The surface is inked by a roller.

Sheet-fed offset Sheet-fed offset presses range from the small machines used in instant print shops which print A4 size, up to large book presses which can print double A0 size. They may print only one colour or up to six colours. Some machines (called "perfectors") can print both sides of the sheet in one operation.

Most multi-colour presses print four colours and are used for four-colour process work (printing black, cyan, yellow and magenta).

Web-fed offset Most web-offset presses are "blanket-to-blanket"; that is, the web of paper runs between the two blanket cylinders so that both sides are printed simultaneously, with each of the blanket cylinders acting as the impression cylinder to the other.

Many web-offset presses are designed to print an A4 product, as this is the size of most magazines and catalogues. These presses print 16, 32 or 64 pages at a time.

Web-offset machines fold the paper as they print and, with high printing speeds, this means that where colour is being printed, the ink has to be dried before folding to prevent "set-off" (smudging). The drying is done by passing the printed web of paper through a tunnel before folding. There are several methods of drying, and these include gas-flame, hot air, ultra-violet and infra-red.

Despite their high speed, web-offset presses can produce good quality. In fact, the drying facility on web presses means that a thicker film of ink can be carried than on sheet-fed presses, giving more depth and gloss. Also, many web presses can give extra gloss by the use of a silicone applicator after printing.

Web-offset machines are used to print magazines, holiday brochures, some books, mail-order catalogues and long-run (30,000-plus) brochures. Many newspapers, both local and national, have switched in recent years from letterpress to web-offset, which gives better quality reproduction of photographs, offers colour, and links more readily with modern typesetting methods.

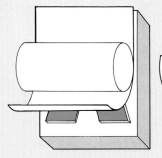

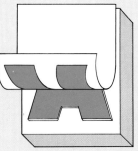

Paper is placed over the inked image and pressed onto it by an impression cylinder.

The final printed image.

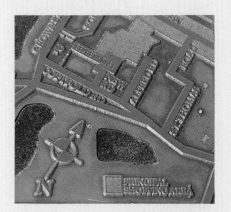

area which is clear on the negative is hardened by the light and therefore becomes resistant to corrosion by acid. When the plate is etched, the acid etches the non-image area to below the image area so that it does not print.

Letterpress blocks can be made for four-colour process printing from negatives separated on cameras or scanners as for offset lithography.

A letterpress block (above) is made by photosensitizing a piece of copper or zinc and exposing it under a negative. The image

LETTERPRESS Letterpress was overtaken in the 1960s and eventually replaced as the main printing process by offset. The reasons for this include the high cost of metal type and blocks; the greater cost of the papers required to give a good result; the relatively slow speed of most letterpress machines; and the fact that modern methods of origination (for both text and pictures) do not lend themselves to the creation of a raised surface.

However, there are still several areas in which letterpress is used successfully. These include private-press work (from metal type), business forms, labels and computer stationery.

Letterpress presses The platen press is used for small jobs (maximum size A3) and consists of two flat surfaces of metal, hinged at the bottom, which are brought together under pressure to make the impression. The forme with the type and blocks is fixed onto one surface and inked by rollers and the paper is placed on the other surface. The platen press can be used for small "jobbing" work such as letterheads, tickets and small leaflets, although most of this work is now done on small offset presses. Platen presses are, however, still used for embossing, cutting and creasing, and hot-foil blocking.

The flat-bed cylinder press holds the forme in a flat metal bed while the ink rollers and sheets of paper roll over it alternately. The paper is held round

---

LETTERPRESS

Advantages
Dense ink
Good printing of type for high-quality books
No problems with ink/water balance
Less paper wastage than other processes

Disadvantages
High cost of printing surface
More expensive paper needed to get same results as other processes
Sheet-fed machines run slowly
Modern origination methods suit other processes better

a cylinder while it is pressed on the forme to make the impression. At one time most books and magazines were printed on this type of press. Nowadays, they are used by private presses for high-quality limited edition bookwork.

The rotary press prints from a curved or flexible metal or plastic plate, which is clamped on a cylinder which revolves against another cylinder carrying the paper. Rotary presses can be sheet-fed or web-fed and where letterpress is still used, it is mainly now on rotary presses.

GRAVURE Before the invention of modern gravure methods, artists had used a similar method of printing to produce etchings, in which the image was etched into a copper plate, filled with ink and printed on flat-bed presses. The introduction of photogravure (also known as rotogravure) dates from the use of photographic methods, in which the printing surface is produced from film.

Gravure is an "intaglio" process; that is, the printing image is recessed into the plate, rather than being flat (as in lithography) or raised (as in letter-press). The image consists of cells engraved into a copper-plated plate or cylinder. These cells are filled with liquid ink and the cells vary in depth so that they will leave the required amount of ink on the various parts of the printed image. A blade (known as a doctor blade) is pulled across the surface of the plate or cylinder to remove excess ink. The paper is fed through the press on an electrostatic rubber-covered cylinder which presses the paper into the recesses to pick up the ink.

The ink is very thin and, being spirit-based, dries through evaporation immediately after printing. Unlike web-offset, therefore, the process does not need elaborate drying arrangements.

The gravure press Most gravure printing is done on web-fed machines, using reels of paper and folding on press. The machines are usually very large, printing up to 128 pages of A4 size and running at speeds of up to 50,000 an hour. Sheet-fed gravure presses are used for stamps and very high quality photographic books, but there are very few of these presses still running.

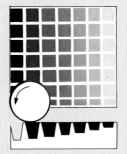

Gravure is an intaglio process, which means that the printing image is recessed into the plate and filled with ink. The cells vary in depth but not in size (left).

Because of the cell structure, type can look fuzzy in smaller sizes, as the cell walls break up the fine detail. Yet gravure printing of photographs is often superior to other processes as it gives a true "halftone" effect in which the darker areas of the photograph actually carry more ink as they are printed from deeper cells.

Photographs printed by gravure have greater contrast between light and dark areas, as a heavy film of ink is carried. Gravure can also give good results on quite cheap papers.

The reason why gravure is mainly used for very long runs is that the plates and cylinders are very expensive to buy and prepare and this high start-up cost can only be recovered from a long run.

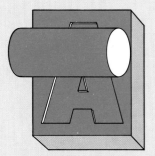

The printing image is recessed and ink is applied by a roller. It fills the cells and some remains on the surface.

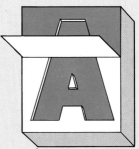

A thin, flexible steel blade (a doctor blade) is drawn across the plate to remove excess ink from the non-printing areas.

GRAVURE

Uses of gravure Gravure is used for very long-run (300,000 copies or more) magazines (such as newspaper colour supplements) and mail order catalogues. It is also used for some kinds of packaging, printing on cellophane, decorative laminates, and wallpaper.

SCREEN PRINTING In screen printing, a stencil cut by hand or made photographically (see pages 20-21) is supported on a screen of synthetic fibre or metal. In the early days of the process, the screen was made of silk and the process known as silk-screen printing.

The screen is stretched over a frame of wood or metal, and ink is spread along the screen by means of a rubber squeegee, which squeezes the ink through the screen in the image areas. The stencil prevents ink going through in the non-image (background) areas.

The screen-printing press Many screen presses are manually operated, as regards both the feeding of the paper and the application of the ink. These presses consist of a simple frame hinged to a flat surface. The advantage of this type of equipment is that it is very cheap and so lends itself to printing at home, or the printing of posters by community groups. Artists can also produce original prints on this type of equipment.

In semi-automatic presses, the screen is raised and lowered automatically and the squeegee operation is

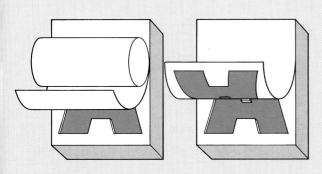

The paper is put on the plate and pressed against it by a roller. The pressure forces the paper into the cells to pick up the ink.

The final printed image.

In the "litho-to-gravure" conversion technique, proofs are produced as for litho and can be Matchprints or Cromalins or wet proofs. The designer corrects these in exactly the same way as litho proofs and the repro house carries out the corrections before making the opalines. It is expensive to correct the cylinders once made, but it can be done by chemical methods. The chemicals etch the cells to make them deeper to give stronger colour, or fill them in to make them shallower and give

weaker colour. The latter is more difficult.

Gravure is a specialized process and even more than in litho, it is important for the designer to work closely with the repro house and printer, as techniques of gravure reproduction and printing can vary from one supplier to another much more than in the relatively standardized litho process.

Litho-to-gravure proofs always look a little flatter, as the conversion entails some loss of highlights.

Regardless of the printing process used, the paper can be fed into the press either as sheets or reels of paper. When paper is made it comes off the papermaking machine in very large reels. Where printing is to be sheet-fed, this paper is slit on the reel and then cut up into sheets of the required size. The feeder on the press picks up the sheets with a combination of metal fingers and vacuum

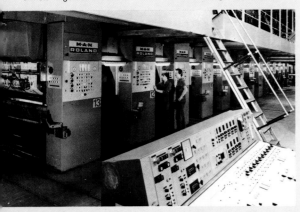

suckers and feeds them through to be printed. After printing, the flat sheets are folded on a separate machine.

In web-fed (also known as reel-fed) printing, the paper is supplied to the machine in the form of reels. These can be as wide as 4m (13ft) on some presses. The front end of the press has a reelstand, which holds the paper as it is unwound and fed through the press. The

method of making the impression is the same as with a sheet-fed press, but the web-fed press runs much faster because the machine is not slowed down by having to pick up and put down each sheet. Most web presses can fold on press and some can also glue, perforate or wire-stitch.

The advantages of web-fed printing are: speed (15,000 to 40,000 impressions per hour compared with 5,000 to 12,000 for sheet-fed printing); the fact that folding can be done as an in-line operation; and savings can be made by buying paper in reels rather than sheets. The disadvantages are that web-fed machines have a much higher capital cost and a longer make-ready time (see opposite) and most machines can only produce items of a fixed length. Also, web-fed presses waste more paper than sheet-fed, both during make-ready and running, due to the higher speed.

also automatic, but the paper or other material to be printed is inserted and removed by hand.

Screen-printing machines often have vacuum bases to help separate the paper from the screen after printing. Fully automatic presses also feed and deliver the stock automatically and some have an impression cylinder which holds the paper while the screen moves in unison and the squeegee remains stationary. Automatic presses can print at up to 6,000 impressions an hour.

Because of the thick film of ink used, drying can be a problem and on short runs the sheets are laid out to dry on racks. However, it is quite common for automatic machines to have drying tunnels or ultra-violet drying units.

Uses of screen printing As the process can apply a thick layer of ink and print large sheets of paper, it is ideal for posters. The screen process can print on virtually any material including wood, fabric, glass, plastic and metal. Screen printing is the process used for plastic and metal signs, bottles, transfers and printed circuits. It can also print on very light papers, such as sewing patterns, which would cause feeding problems in other processes.

FLEXOGRAPHY This is a derivative of the letterpress process, using flexible relief plates and thin, fluid inks that dry by evaporation (sometimes assisted by heat). The plates are made from either rubber or photopolymer with the image raised as in conventional letterpress.

The flexographic press Most presses for flexography are web-fed. Ink is applied to the plate by a metal "anilox" roller with cells etched into it, which carry the ink and transfer it to the plate. Machines can be multi-colour for four-colour process work.

Uses of flexography Flexography is mainly used for packaging (see pages 134–137) – printing on cellophane, plastic and metallic foils. It can in fact be used for virtually any material that will physically pass through the press. It is also used for some local

SCREEN PRINTING
Advantages
Can print a heavy film of ink
Economical for short runs (even below 100 copies)
Can print on virtually any material
Disadvantages
Difficult to achieve fine detail
Low output
Drying requirements

and national newspapers, although offset is gaining ground in this field because it reproduces black and white and colour photographs better and makes type sharper.

Although most mass-market paperback books are printed offset, some suppliers still successfully print by flexography, using photopolymer plates.

Flexography used to be the poor relation of the other processes, but improvements in plates and inks are ensuring its growth.

FOIL BLOCKING AND EMBOSSING Although not strictly speaking a printing process, because it forms part of the binding or finishing operation, foil blocking is in common use on promotional items of print and book covers and jackets.

Blocking and embossing are done on converted letterpress machines of either the platen or flat-bed type and the image is carried on a brass which has a raised surface and is made in the same way as a letterpress block (see page 25). The brass is fixed on the bed or platen, which is heated, and then the brass is pressed into a ribbon of foil. The combination of heat and pressure detaches the metallic foil from its carrier ribbon and applies it to the paper, creating a three-dimensional effect at the same time. "Blind" embossing is done in very much the same manner, but without the use of foil.

Because blocking and embossing are fairly crude

processes, the designer should not attempt to use too much fine detail or small type as it may well get squashed. Simple designs and bold type work best. Finally, do bear in mind that finishing can extend the schedule.

MAKE-READY In all printing processes make-ready must be carried out before printing can begin. The operation includes setting up the press to accept the size and thickness of paper being used, putting the printing plates on, changing the ink if necessary, adjusting the folder (on a web-fed press), ensuring that the colour is the right strength and that the image is in the correct position.

Make-ready is important because good quality depends on it. Also, because presses are not producing while making ready, make-ready forms an important part of the cost of printing.

Rubber duplicate plates (below) for printing a paperback book by flexography. Each page is a separate rubber plate and is fixed with adhesive to a plastic foil base.

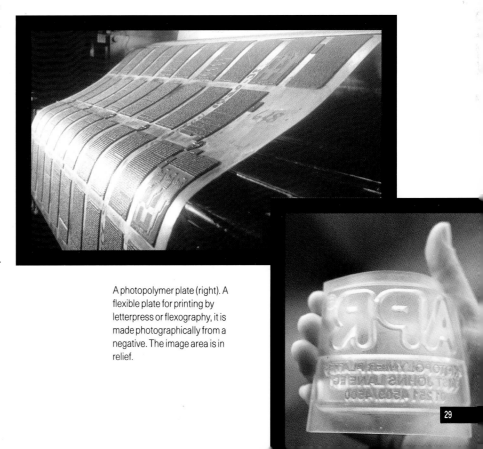

A photopolymer plate (right). A flexible plate for printing by letterpress or flexography, it is made photographically from a negative. The image area is in relief.

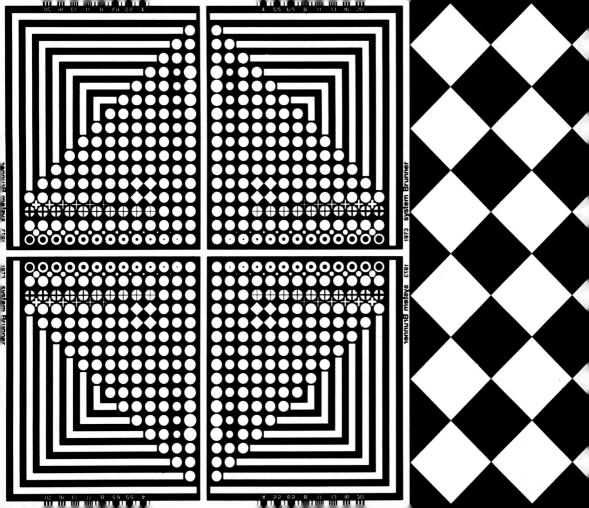

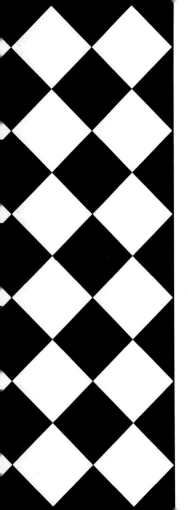

ALL ABOUT

This section explains the basic principles of how originals are presented to the repro house and what the four-colour process can achieve. Paper, dot gain, undercolour removal and moiré are all explained in detail.

The different methods of proofing are shown, as well as how the repro house produces final film and carries out corrections.

PROOFS

1

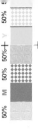

What do I need to tell the repro house about the printer?

Once the design of a job has been completed, it takes the work of the repro house and printer to bring it to a successful conclusion. It is absolutely vital that there is good communication between the three parties at this stage, rather than each working independently.

In some cases, one company will carry out both the reproduction and printing and here the designer can safely leave it to the company to communicate internally. However, in most cases the reproduction and printing are carried out by separate companies and it is up to the designer or production department to ensure that each company knows what is required of the other. If this is not done, the result could be a job on which the proofs look excellent, but where it is impossible to obtain the same result on the final printed work.

The main means of communicating the required information is the printer's specification sheet. This tells the repro house what the printer requires as regards: screen ruling, paper type, dot shape, dot gain, ink densities, minimum and maximum dot sizes, undercolour removal (if required), type of colour bar.

Other information which the printer might give includes: lay-down sheets (showing trims and bleeds), imposition scheme (showing where pages fall), plate specifications (if the repro house is supplying plates rather than film), type of film (negative or positive and right-reading or wrong-reading when viewed with the emulsion side down).

In addition to the specification sheet, if a job poses particular problems, it is a good idea for the designer to set up a meeting with the repro house and printer to look at the layouts and originals, before reproduction starts.

The repro house should be advised if the job is to be varnished or laminated.

PRINTER'S SPECIFICATION SHEET

On specification sheets, check the dot gain and ink densities. These can vary from one printer to another, as can the proofing sequence.

A PRINTER

Reproduction requirements for sheet-fed offset

COLOUR BAR	Gretag CMS2 control strip						
DENSITOMETER	Gretag			80%		40%	
DENSITY READINGS	COLOUR	DENSITY	TOL.	DOT GAIN	TOL.	DOT GAIN	TOL.
GLOSS ART PAPER	CYAN	1.45	±0.10	9	±2	14	±3
	MAGENTA	1.40	±0.10	9	±2	14	±3
	YELLOW	1.40	±0.10	10	±2	16	±3
	BLACK	1.85	±0.15	10	±2	16	±3
MATT COATED	CYAN	1.35	±0.10	10	±3	15	±4
	MAGENTA	1.30	±0.10	10	±3	15	±4
	YELLOW	1.30	±0.10	11	±3	17	±4
	BLACK	1.75	±0.15	11	±3	17	±4
UNCOATED	CYAN	1.20	±0.10	14	±4	21	±5
	MAGENTA	1.15	±0.10	14	±4	21	±5
	YELLOW	1.20	±0.10	14	±4	21	±5
	BLACK	1.55	±0.15	15	±4	22	±5

PROOFING SEQUENCE – Cyan, Magenta, Yellow, Black

DOT SHAPE – Elliptic

PERCENTAGE OF UNDERCOLOUR REMOVAL – CYAN 85%
– MAGENTA 75%
– YELLOW 75%
– BLACK 95%

SCREEN RULING – 150

INK – British Standard BS 4666

FILM – Positive film right-reading emulsion-down. 4 thou thick

```
                                    Op
                    40253a
L000
  Spec-check
  FACE
  DPS: Overall gutter loss - 10mm
  Pub.Co.:  Wagadon Ltd
  Address:  The Old Laundry
  (Copy)    Ossington Buildings
            Off Moxon Street
            LONDON W1
  Contact:  Rod Sopp
  Tel:      01-935 8232      DPS: 283 x 444
  Page  Type: 283 x 212      DPS: 313 x 474
  Page  Bleed: 313 x 242     DPS: 303 x 464
  Page  Trim: 303 x 232 or 138 x 210
  Half  Type: 281 x 102 or     x
  Half  Bleed:      x    or     x    or
  Half  Trim: 138 x 102 or     x        or
  Qtr   Page:       x      Mini:      x
                       Length:
  Display Cols:           ,    ,    ,
    Col Widths:    ',  Length:
  Class. Cols:           ,    ',  ',  '
    Col Widths:    ',  9' Spec-check Index
  £ to continue...
```

```
                                    Op
                    40253b
L000
  Spec-check
  THE FACE
  Printed: Web Offset
  Binding: Perfect
  Paper Wght: Text-80gsm  Cvrs-135gsm
       Make: T-Kaukas     C-Kaukas
  Publ.Date: Monthly 3/4th Thurs prec.
  Display copy dates:-
  Mech + Trans B&W- 3 weeks Col- 3 weeks
  Final Film   B&W- 3 weeks Col- 3 weeks
  Class. copy dates:-
               B&W- n/a
  Printer: Severn Valley Printers
  Nearest Red Star: Cardiff

  Copy Required:-
  B&W:   Bromides/Artwork + Cont Tone/
         Film: Positives RRE Down
  Colour: Artwork + Transparencies/
          Film: Positives RRE Down
  Screen Size:   48 B&W    54 Colour
  Method Of Punching: n/a
  £ to continue          9 Spec-check Index
```

```
                                    Op
                    40253c
L000
  Spec-check
  THE FACE
                 Y     C     M     B
                      75    45    15
  Screen Angles: 90   1.3   1.3   1.8
  Density:       1.1
  Dot Gain: 18% in 40%, 14% in 75%
  UCR: Between 200% and 270%
  Proofing Method: n/a
  No. Of Proofs Required: n/a
  Colour Sequence: n/a
  Proof Direction: n/a

  Special Instructions:

  Inserts:-
  - Loose: Size        ) Available on
           Weight      ) Application
  - Bound: Size        )
           Weight      )
           Guard Width )
                       9 Spec-check Index
```

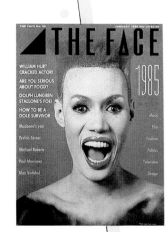

Repro specification sheet (left) for *The Face*.

The annual guide *BRAD* lists UK periodical publications with printers' specifications.

RRE This means the film supplied by the printer will be positive. RRE stands for Right Reading Emulsion down. Sometimes a spec will state WRE, which means Wrong Reading Emulsion down. Whether RRE or WRE is chosen depends on the printing process.

Density These figures represent the ink densities the printer runs its press at to give the optimum results. Ink densities vary depending on what is being printed – for example a newspaper would be printed on .7 for all colours.

UCR This stands for undercolour removal. The range of figures given here represents the combined percentages of the four colours with UCR. If the printer specifies a maximum of 270% the individual percentages of each colour will be: cyan 65% + yellow 55% + magenta 55% + black 95% = 270% maximum.

Screen angles This part of the spec shows the angle for each colour used by the printer.

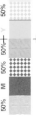

What can the scanner correct on a bad original?

THERE ARE MANY WAYS in which the scanner can correct a bad original. The main thing is that the designer should point out the fault to the repro house and say what result is required. It helps the repro house if the designer sends a sample to be matched when he returns the marked-up colour proofs. In fact, it is best if a sample is supplied with the original, whether this is good or bad. If the repro house is given a bad original with no instructions, it will assume that the task is to match the proof to the original.

The scanner can adjust exposure levels and contrast and remove colour casts. However, any correction done on the scanner will affect the whole area of the original. Localized correction will involve either retouching by hand or the use of an electronic page make-up system, both of which can be expensive.

It is not really possible to correct a transparency which is too grainy. In this case the designer will have to either find a new original for the subject or accept a result similar to the original.

Is it possible to improve detail?
To achieve what the designer wants here, the repro house will increase shadows and weak midtones to give a better range to the picture. A slight increase of yellow and black in blues/violets will neutralize the blue cast in the shadows. The increase in the shadows will probably be in the yellow, which will also make the browns in the rocks a richer colour. This example shows how much improvement the repro house can achieve.

BAD EXPOSURE

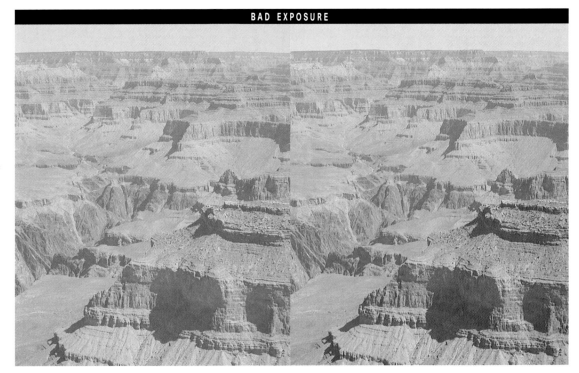

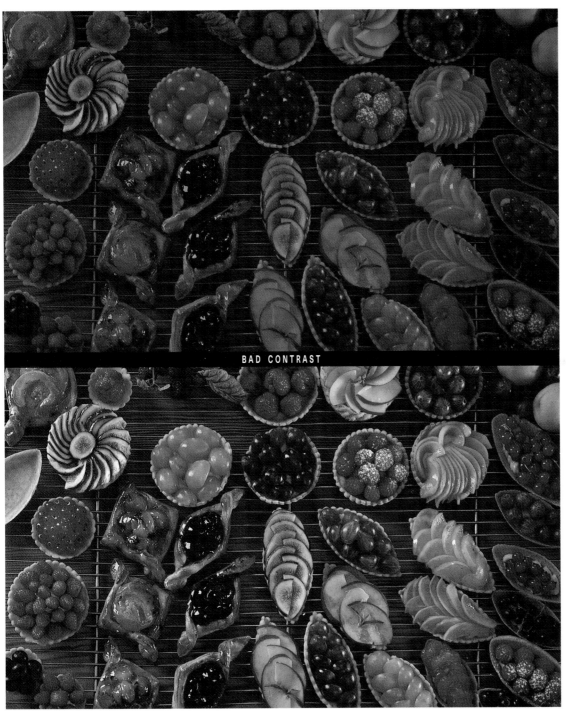

BAD CONTRAST

Can the contrast be improved?
To improve on this original, the repro house will increase the highlights to give better modelling. Doing this will probably make the catchlights on the metal blow out to white, but this cannot be avoided.

Also, a reduction in the midtones will allow the colours to come through and "open out" the picture. The black highlight can also be reduced to brighten the picture. Again, a great improvement on the original.

Note that the repro house will always try to match the transparency, unless asked to do otherwise, so if the designer wants a change or improvement, it must be requested before the repro stage.

**Can this image be
made crisper?**
To do this, the repro house will
increase the shadows, to give a
better range. Also, it will increase
the midtones to give the
mountain more contrast with the
white building. Finally, it will
probably increase the highlight
contrast to give slightly more
detail in the building.

Graininess sometimes needs
to be retained as a design
element and here the designer
should alert the repro house to
keep it.

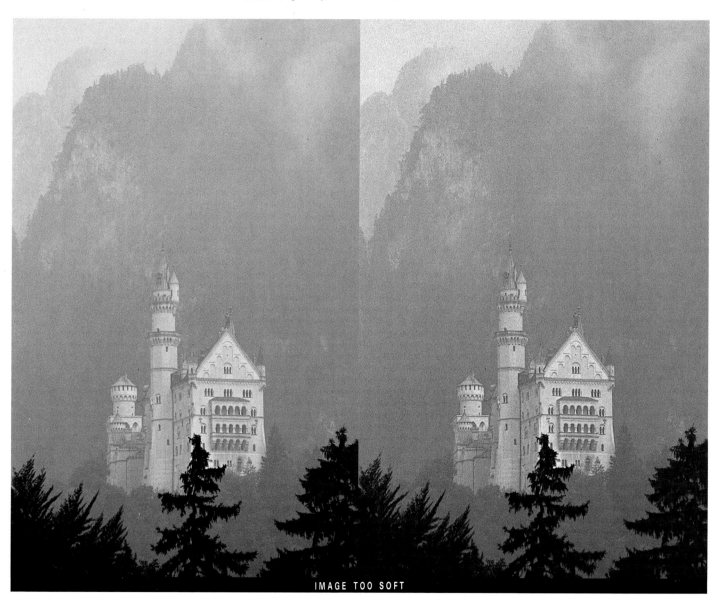

IMAGE TOO SOFT

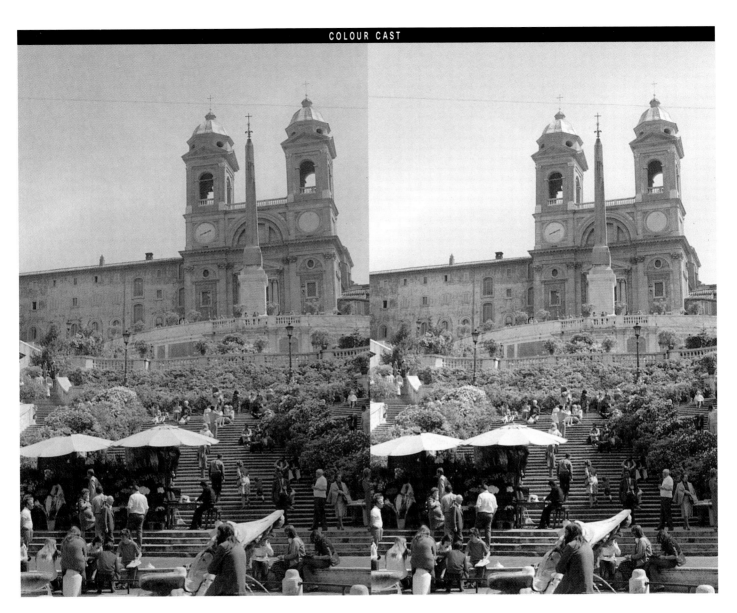

Can repro lose the colour cast?
To lose the colour cast here, the repro house will reduce the cyan and magenta highlights and probably increase the yellow highlights.

The shadows will be made more neutral and the yellow increased in the midtone to make the brickwork warmer and more realistic. It could also be helpful to reduce the cyan midtones, allowing more of the warmth to come through.

There is a marked improvement here, showing what the scanner can achieve.

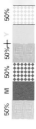

Can the scanner correct a damaged original?

IF THE ORIGINAL is scratched or torn, it can usually be repaired by hand-retouching (putting in dots by hand) or "pixelling" and copy brushing on an electronic page make-up system. Here, the system takes an area adjacent to the damage, measures the colour content and then reproduces it in the affected area.

Both methods can be expensive and the designer should get a price before the repro house starts work, as it may be cheaper to retouch the transparency and make a duplicate.

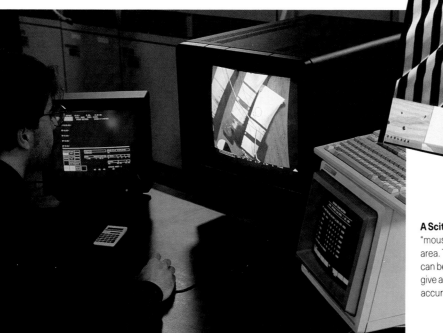

A Scitex operator (left) uses the "mouse" to retouch the required area. The area he is working on can be enlarged on the screen to give a greater degree of accuracy.

The torn original (above). Before asking the repro house to retouch any damage make sure you are quoted a price. Sometimes it may be cheaper to make a duplicate transparency and retouch that. Some electronic page make-up systems have the facility to output a repaired transparency.

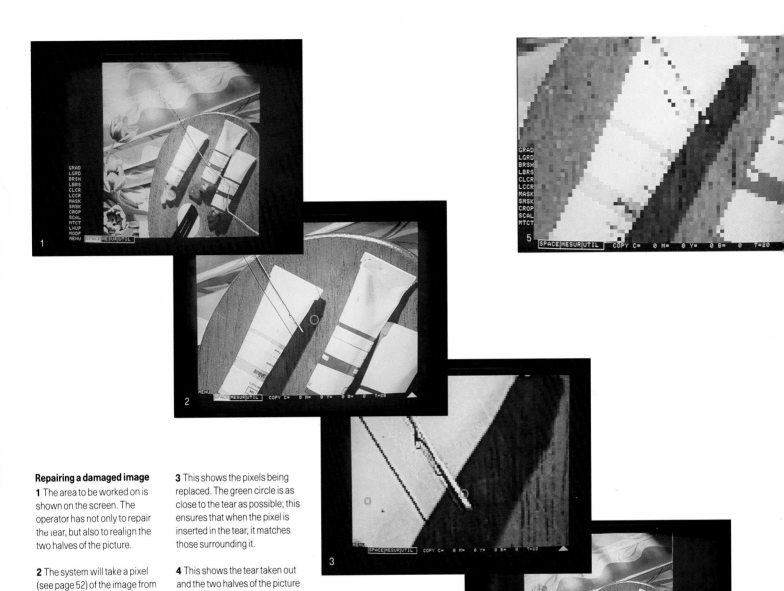

Repairing a damaged image

1 The area to be worked on is shown on the screen. The operator has not only to repair the tear, but also to realign the two halves of the picture.

2 The system will take a pixel (see page 52) of the image from the green circle and duplicate it in the damaged area.

3 This shows the pixels being replaced. The green circle is as close to the tear as possible; this ensures that when the pixel is inserted in the tear, it matches those surrounding it.

4 This shows the tear taken out and the two halves of the picture realigned.

5 This is a 4,000 times enlargement showing the individual pixels.

How much can an image be enlarged without loss of quality?

THE DESIGNER should be aware that different photographic films have different characteristics and some can bear enlargement better than others. Some 35mm films, for example, have a lot more grain than others, which may not show on the transparency but becomes much more apparent when enlarged.

As a general rule, it is best not to enlarge a 35mm transparency by more than 1000% (×10). Square 55mm transparencies do not have the same problems with grain as 35mm. However, they can hold a lot of detail that only becomes apparent on enlargement (such as hairs on a face).

Certain subjects, such as jewellery or food photography, can bear enlargement well. The reason is that these are normally shot in a studio under controlled lighting conditions.

If a subject has been enlarged too much, then the only thing that can be done at the colour proof stage to get a better quality image is to redesign the picture smaller and rescan it.

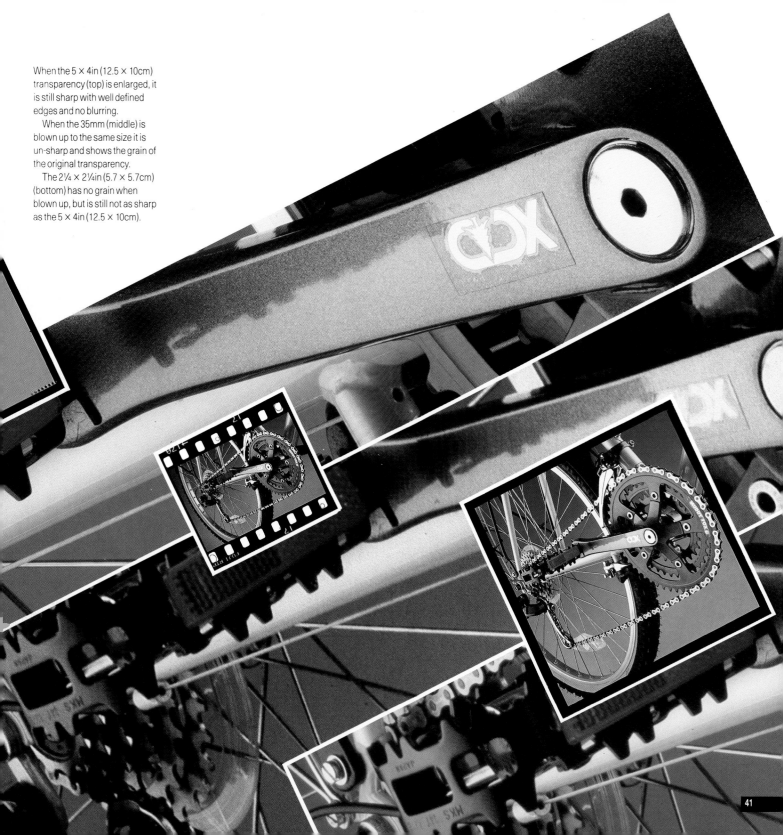

When the 5 × 4in (12.5 × 10cm)
transparency (top) is enlarged, it
is still sharp with well defined
edges and no blurring.

When the 35mm (middle) is
blown up to the same size it is
un-sharp and shows the grain of
the original transparency.

The 2¼ × 2¼in (5.7 × 5.7cm)
(bottom) has no grain when
blown up, but is still not as sharp
as the 5 × 4in (12.5 × 10cm).

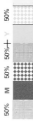

How should flat artwork be presented to the repro house?

MOST SCANNERS have a drum around which the original is wrapped, so the flat artwork needs to be on a flexible board. If this is not possible, there are three ways of reproducing it. First, where artwork is painted on a rigid board, the repro house can peel off the top surface to make it flexible. This can lead to creasing or other damage. In particular, poster paints are very brittle and when bent can crack and flake off.

Secondly, the rigid artwork can be reproduced with a process camera. The problem here is that the process camera (which preceded the scanner as a method of separation) is slow and expensive and lacks sophisticated electronic controls. Also, most repro houses no longer have process cameras for colour separation.

Where artwork cannot be flexible, it is probably best to make a colour transparency from it and scan it in the normal way. This particularly applies when the original is valuable or is painted with poster paints.

Another reproduction problem with flat artwork occurs when strong solid colours (particularly fluorescent) are used by the artist. There are some colours which cannot be reproduced exactly by the four-colour process. The designer can check this before reproduction by using a four-colour tint chart to see how closely the colour can be matched.

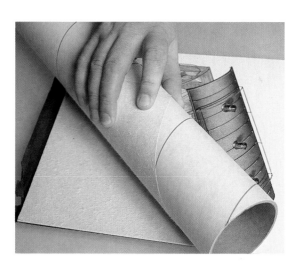

Flat artwork Try to avoid artwork which has to be peeled, because of the danger of damage. If an artwork is too valuable to risk damage, a transparency should be made, either 5 × 4 in (12.5 × 10 cm) or 10 × 8 in (25 × 20 cm). A transparency should also be made when the artwork is too big for the scanner. The transparency should include a grey scale and a colour scale.

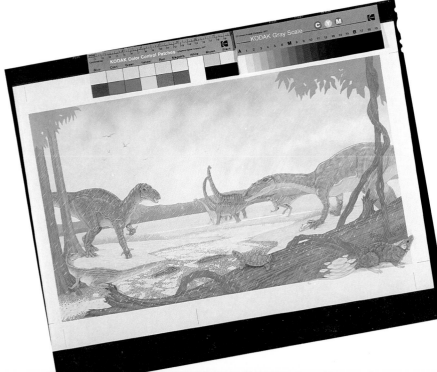

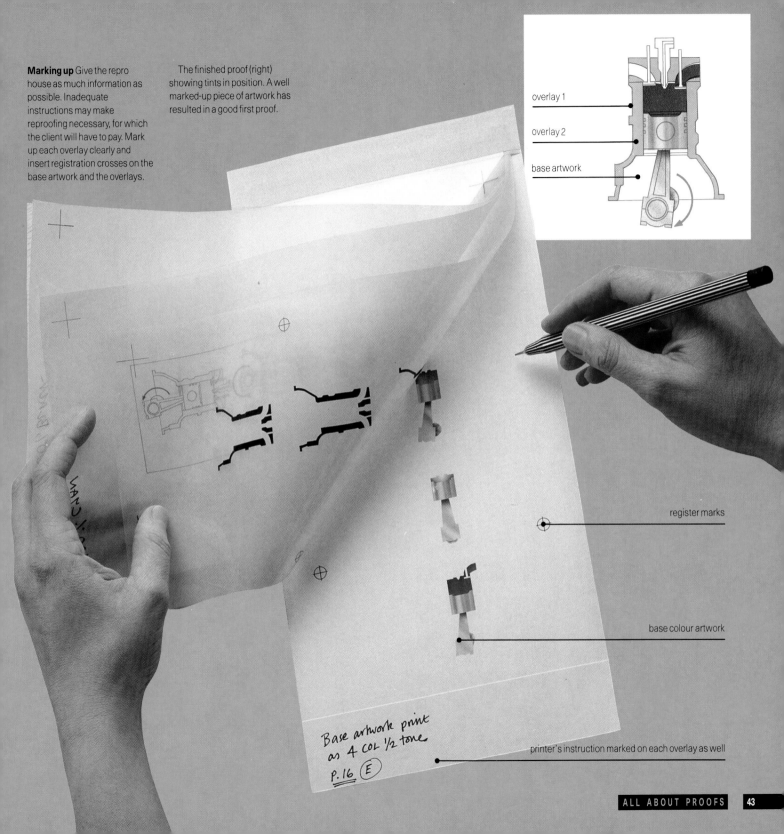

Marking up Give the repro house as much information as possible. Inadequate instructions may make reproofing necessary, for which the client will have to pay. Mark up each overlay clearly and insert registration crosses on the base artwork and the overlays.

The finished proof (right) showing tints in position. A well marked-up piece of artwork has resulted in a good first proof.

overlay 1

overlay 2

base artwork

register marks

base colour artwork

Base artwork print
as 4 COL ½ tone
P. 16 E

printer's instruction marked on each overlay as well

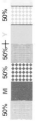

Are some colours impossible to match using the four-colour process?

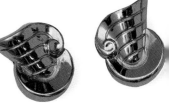

NEITHER PHOTOGRAPHY nor colour separation are perfect processes. The subject shot by the photographer has an infinite range of colours which is condensed on the transparency and further condensed in colour separation. Four-colour printing is therefore an approximation to the transparency, which itself is an approximation to the original subject. Both processes can get close but can never be perfect.

Normally, the process will come close enough to the original colours to be acceptable. However, serious problems can occur when a proprietary brand uses a special colour that is difficult or impossible to match in the four-colour process.

In general, the most difficult colours to reproduce are golds, deep blues and certain greens. Some companies admit in their specifications that the corporate colours cannot be exactly matched out of the four process colours.

Jewellery Gold, silver and some precious stones (right) are difficult to match for colour. Make sure that transparencies are as sharp as possible, as this will give good definition and detail.

Pantone Process Colour Simulator This shows special Pantone colours and their equivalents made up using tints of the four process colours. As you can see, the four-colour process is unable to match the extra quality and range of colour that the Pantone special colour system offers.

PANTONE Process Color Simulator 747XR

PANTONE Process Color Simulator 747XR

cyan scale
0-100% right to left

C   M

80

100

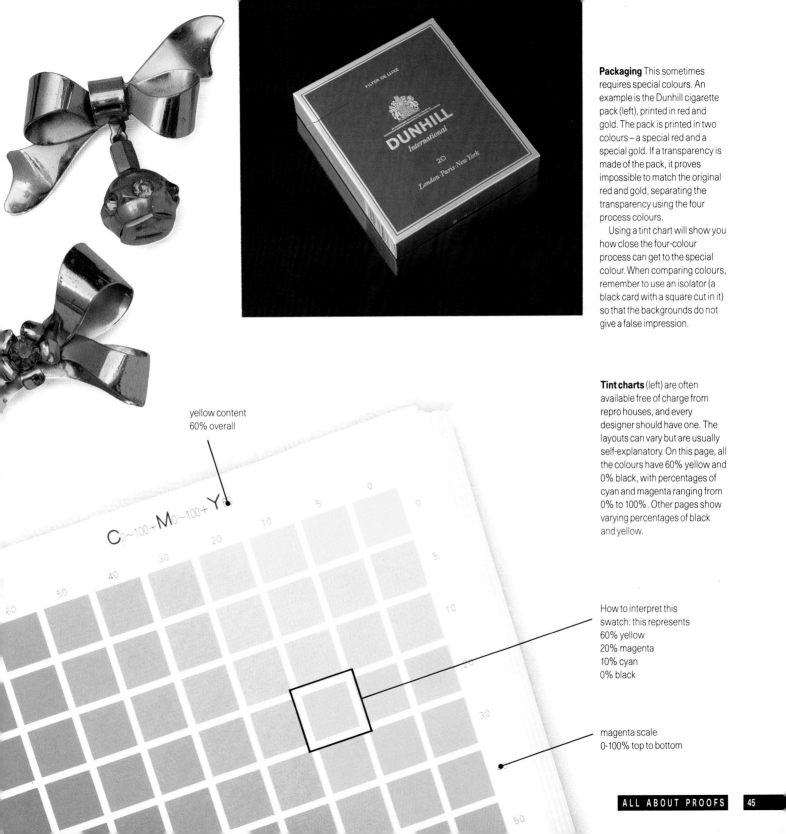

Packaging This sometimes requires special colours. An example is the Dunhill cigarette pack (left), printed in red and gold. The pack is printed in two colours – a special red and a special gold. If a transparency is made of the pack, it proves impossible to match the original red and gold, separating the transparency using the four process colours.

Using a tint chart will show you how close the four-colour process can get to the special colour. When comparing colours, remember to use an isolator (a black card with a square cut in it) so that the backgrounds do not give a false impression.

Tint charts (left) are often available free of charge from repro houses, and every designer should have one. The layouts can vary but are usually self-explanatory. On this page, all the colours have 60% yellow and 0% black, with percentages of cyan and magenta ranging from 0% to 100%. Other pages show varying percentages of black and yellow.

yellow content
60% overall

C₀~100+M₀~100+Y

How to interpret this swatch: this represents
60% yellow
20% magenta
10% cyan
0% black

magenta scale
0-100% top to bottom

What are undercolour removal and achromatic reproduction?

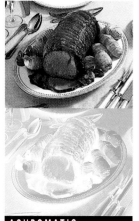

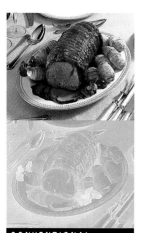

ACHROMATIC

CONVENTIONAL

In UNDERCOLOUR REMOVAL the grey and neutral tones in the magenta, cyan and yellow are removed and replaced with black. The main reason for doing this is that black ink is cheaper than the other three colours. Also, the less the weight of ink carried overall, the more control is possible on the press.

In conventional undercolour removal, most of the colour and tone is still contributed by the three primary colours, with the black lending only deeper shadow tones. In achromatic reproduction, the very minimum amount of each colour required is computed and the black added to produce the required depth of colour. The process is intended to give no bias in the shadow areas and using it will help to avoid "tracking" problems (see page 141), particularly when matching up two halves of a double-page spread. This is because the cyan, magenta and yellow carry less ink and are therefore easier to control. Achromatic reproduction is still considered unproven and the designer should not specify it unless it is proposed by the client or printer.

Overcoming tracking problems With ordinary repro and printing, any unexpected increase in the complementary colour on press can affect the job. With achromatic repro the complementary colours are reduced so that this is unlikely to affect any hues of colour. The example above shows the difference between a conventional and an achromatic print. Compare the two cyan separations – the achromatic set shows hardly any blue. Thus the joint of meat in the finished achromatic print has a truer colour than that of the meat in the conventional tint example.

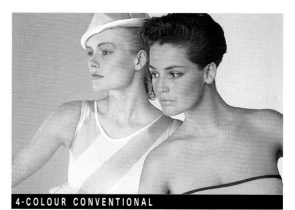

4-COLOUR CONVENTIONAL

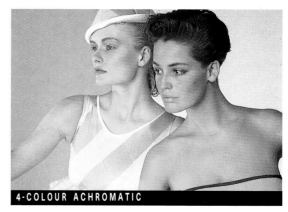

4-COLOUR ACHROMATIC

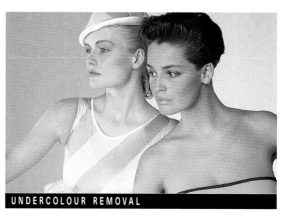

UNDERCOLOUR REMOVAL

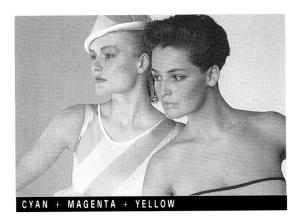

CYAN + MAGENTA + YELLOW

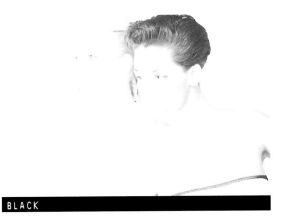

BLACK

Conventional The three colours (cyan, magenta and yellow) make up most of the picture, with black giving density and shape to the shadows and darker colours.

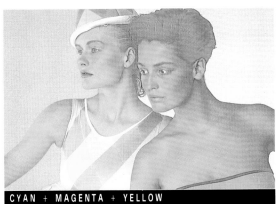

CYAN + MAGENTA + YELLOW

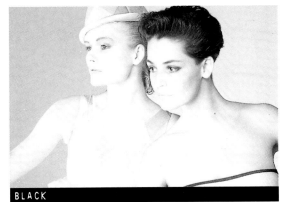

BLACK

Achromatic In achromatic reproduction the complementary colours are reduced as well as the shadows and midtones, and replaced with a greatly increased black.

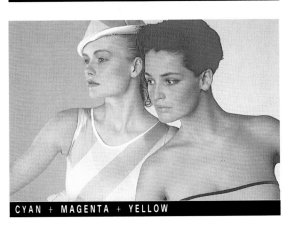

CYAN + MAGENTA + YELLOW

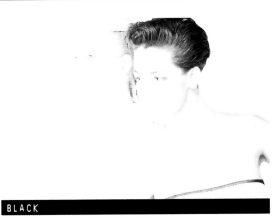

BLACK

Undercolour removal (UCR) UCR is used to subtract equal amounts of cyan, magenta and yellow from shadows and dark degraded colours. These are then replaced by increased black.

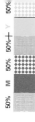

What do I need to know about paper?

THERE IS AN INFINITE variety of papers, from the rather yellow, soggy newsprint used for newspapers to the brilliant white, glossy art paper used for high-quality fashion magazines or art books.

But however good the colour separation may be, the finished result can only be as good as the paper used. A colour separation on newsprint will have dull highlights because the areas that should be white are off-white or grey. Also, the dots used in the separation process sink into the absorbent material and spread. By contrast, on a glossy white art paper, the highlights are bright and the dots lie on the surface and are sharp, giving a crisp, clean result.

Probably the most commonly used paper in publishing and advertising is matt-coated cartridge. This is white and has a surface which is coated to appear matt rather than glossy. The advantage of this is that the surface is smooth enough to give good, sharp reproduction of colour, without the problem of legibility of a gloss paper, which produces reflections that can be an obstacle to reading.

The repro house needs to know the type of paper being used, as the screen rulings and dot gains will be different for different papers. In addition, the repro house should proof on the same type of paper that will be used for the final printed job. If this is not specified, the job might well be proofed on a glossy art paper and printed on an uncoated paper. The printed result would be nowhere near as good as the proof and the client could complain or reject the job, even though uncoated paper was specified in the first place.

Within each type of paper (e.g. uncoated offset, matt-coated cartridge, matt art, gloss art) there are scores of different makes. It can be costly or inconvenient to obtain the actual make of paper to proof on and, although this is the ideal, it is normally sufficient to use the correct type of paper rather than the identical brand on which the job will be printed.

Paper is made in different weights and the proofs should be on the same weight as the final job.

A point to bear in mind is that different papers have different drying times, so some jobs cannot be pushed through quickly at printing stage.

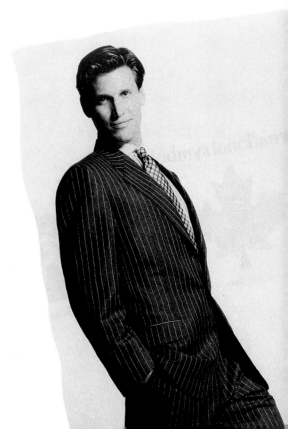

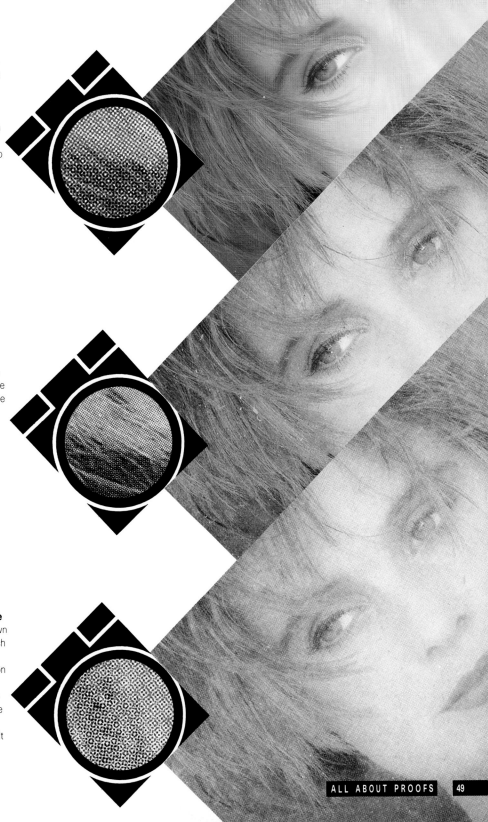

Coated paper used with a fine screen This book is printed on a matt art coated paper, which takes a fairly fine screen (in this case 150) as the ink lies on the surface of the paper, rather than being absorbed and thus spreading, which would give too large a dot.

Showthrough With some lighter papers, lack of opacity can result in "showthrough", which is when the image on the other side of the paper shows through as a dark shadow. It is particularly noticeable (below) when the side you are looking at is mainly white paper and the reverse side is printed with a large, dark area.

Newsprint used with a fine screen Newsprint is very absorbent, and when too fine a screen is used (here it is 150) the ink bleeds into the paper and the dots join together. You can see this clearly in the enlargement.

Newsprint used with a coarse screen Here newsprint is shown with a coarser screen (85) which is much more suitable for this paper. A 65 or 85 screen used on newsprint gives enough room between each dot for the ink to bleed into the paper without the dots joining up. However, the coarser screen makes it difficult to get a good density of colour.

How does screen size affect proofing?

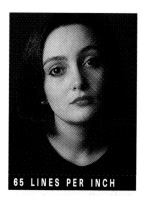
65 LINES PER INCH

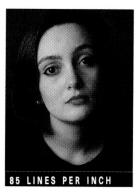
85 LINES PER INCH

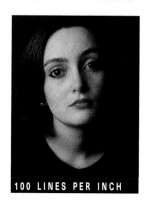
100 LINES PER INCH

Conventional dot shapes
Conventional contact screens are still widely used for mono halftone work. More subtle changes in tonal value are produced by elliptical dot screens compared to square dot screens.

Scanner dot shapes Scanners can produce a range of dot shapes as required, the commonest being square. Dots can be round or elliptical. There is no great difference in quality, though square dots are said to give a better definition if the image being reproduced is, for example, a computer screen.

THE SIZE OF THE DOT in colour separation is governed by the screen ruling. Before scanners were developed, colour separation was carried out using a glass or film screen ruled to make a grid. The light was transmitted through the spaces between the grid lines to create dots of the required size. The screen ruling is therefore the number of lines per inch.

The standard screen rulings are (in lines per inch) 65, 85, 100, 120, 133, 150 and 200. Although the British printing industry normally uses metric measurements, for some reason this has not been applied to screen rulings. In the rest of Europe, however, screens are in lines per centimetre so that 133 per inch, for example, is 54 per centimetre.

The choice of screen ruling depends mainly on the type of paper being used: the rougher the paper, the coarser the screen required. Newspapers printed on newsprint might use 85 screen, on uncoated offset paper 120 or 133 screen, and on matt-coated or art paper 150 screen.

Most publication or advertising colour work is printed on matt-coated or art paper and is therefore 150 screen. If you do not specify a screen ruling, then the repro house will normally work to 150. The screen ruling will be specified in the printer's specification sheet

Although 150 is the finest screen used in normal commercial printing, some printers specialize in the high-quality printing of black and white or colour halftones for photographic books, medical text-books or photographs of coins. Here, screens as fine as 200 or even 300 are used. To reproduce these properly, a very smooth expensive paper is needed.

Standard screens On newsprint the standard screen is 85; most magazines are 133 or 150; high-quality work on good paper can be up to as much as 300. Check whether metric or imperial screen rulings are being used.

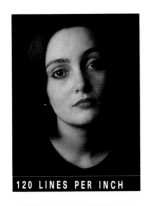

120 LINES PER INCH

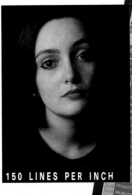

150 LINES PER INCH

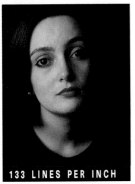

133 LINES PER INCH

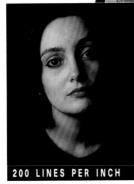

200 LINES PER INCH

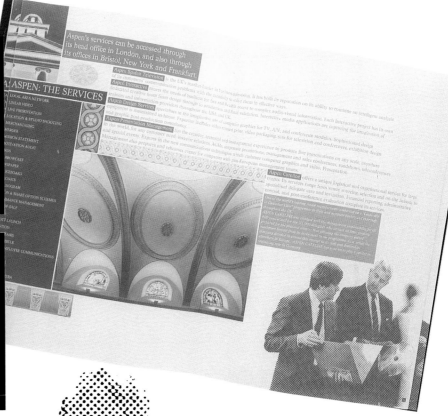

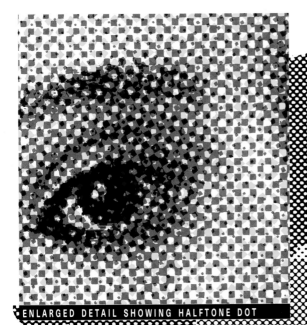

ENLARGED DETAIL SHOWING HALFTONE DOT

Special screens Some screens can be used in the design of the job. You can use mezzo or square line or cut-line screens. Check with your repro house to see if it has these. In the spread (above) two different screen dots have been used to create a textured feel. On the left-hand page, the image was screened at 125, while the image on the right-hand page was screened at 25.

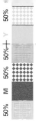

What are scanner effects?

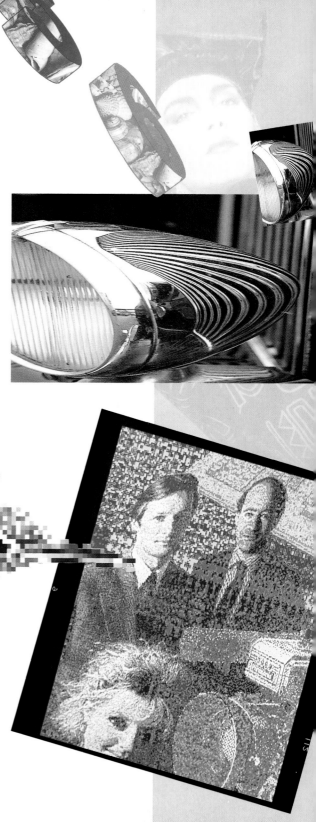

MOST SCANNERS can achieve picture distortion and most electronic page make-up systems can carry out pixellations, vignetting and copy brushing.

When requesting special effects, bear in mind that they can be quite expensive and ask the repro house to quote a price before starting work.

Distortion These two examples of distortion (right and far right) show just what can be achieved using this scanning technique. The female model has been squeezed by about 50%; the chrome headlight has been stretched by 150%.

Ghosting The technique used here (right) involved reproducing an image at a reduced strength of dot, in this case 20%.

Pixellation The word "pixel" comes from PICture ELements, which are the minute image areas created by digitizing a picture. Pixellation means reducing the number of pixels in an image, then enlarging them to give an overall effect. The image of the bird (right) has been pixellated, and the group picture (far right) mixes pixellation with montage techniques.

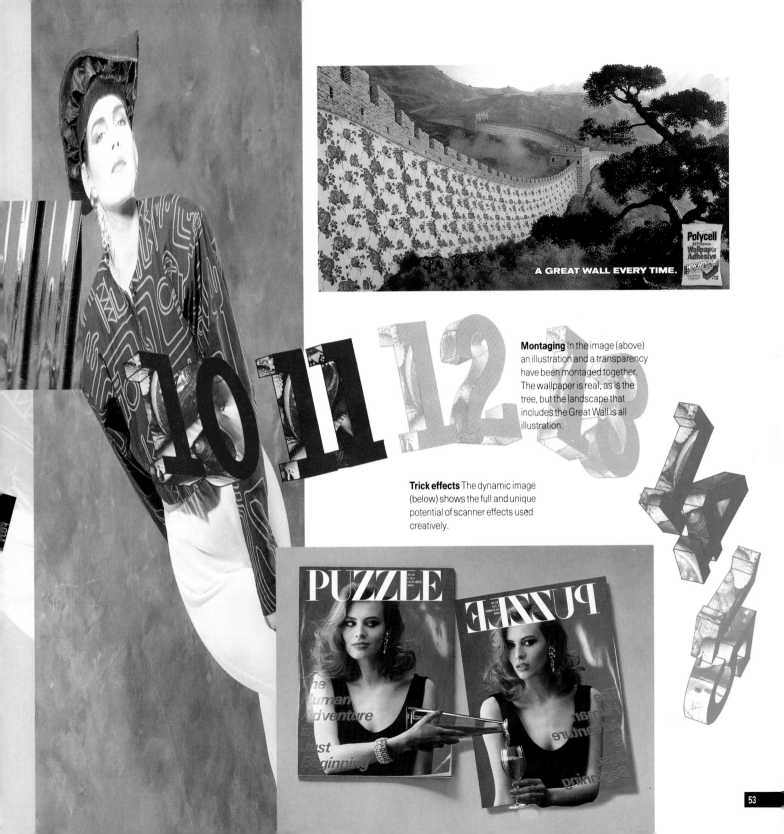

A GREAT WALL EVERY TIME.

Polycell All Purpose Wallpaper Adhesive NOW WITH PVA

Montaging In the image (above) an illustration and a transparency have been montaged together. The wallpaper is real, as is the tree, but the landscape that includes the Great Wall is all illustration.

Trick effects The dynamic image (below) shows the full and unique potential of scanner effects used creatively.

PUZZLE

The Human Adventure is Just Beginning

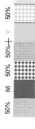

How are final films produced?

Where the repro house does not have an electronic page make-up system, the following methods are used to arrive at final film. First the line artwork (CRC) is shot. This film is then given to the scanner operator, who will size the transparency. The transparency is then mounted and scanned.

The job is then passed to a planner, who will "spot" the line negative. This is then taped down onto a sheet of clear plastic foil which has been punched to ensure register with the foils for the other three colours. The planner then plans the negatives of all the colour halftones in one of the four colours. The next stage is to cut masks on a fifth foil to crop the halftones exactly as required and cut masks for any areas of tint appearing. The required tints are then taped at the correct angle to another foil.

The foils are then contacted in a light frame to positive film, using the mask for the halftones laid on top of the halftones for one exposure. The

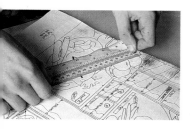

Sizing transparencies It is crucial that the transparency is sized correctly, otherwise it will have to be rescanned. Here, the scanner operator is measuring the distance between two points on the layout.

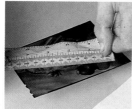

The operator then measures exactly the same points on the transparency. For this, it is important that the original trace is clearly drawn.

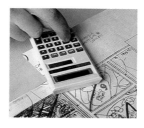

Dividing the required size on the layout by the size on the original gives the percentage enlargement (100% = same size).

Sizing colour transparency

Shooting line artwork

Shooting line The original line artwork (including any type) is shot to the required size on a process camera.

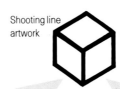

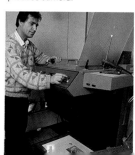

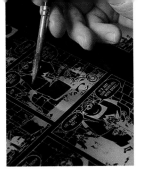

Retouching line film The line negative is spotted out with opaque to eliminate any paste-up marks or dust spots.

Proofing by Matchprint, Cromalin or to make plates for wet proofing

Preparing masks for tints and halftones

Preparing final four-colour positive film

Preparing foil and positioning negative halftone

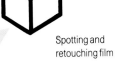

Four-colour scanning

Spotting and retouching film

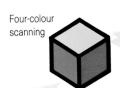

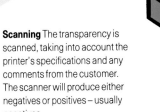

Scanning The transparency is scanned, taking into account the printer's specifications and any comments from the customer. The scanner will produce either negatives or positives – usually negatives.

planner next contacts the foil with the foil of tints and the appropriate mask and makes a second exposure onto the film. Finally, a further mask for register and trim marks is exposed onto the film. At this stage the final film of one of the four colours has been completed.

This final positive film is used as a guide and the other three colours are planned to fit with this and then contacted to the final positive as above, with black type being exposed onto the film for the black. The final films then go for proofing.

ELECTRONIC PAGE MAKE-UP SYSTEMS

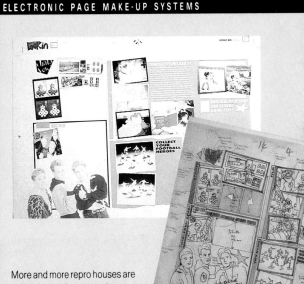

More and more repro houses are using electronic page make-up systems. A typical piece of final film (top) produced by such a system shows all the elements in position. With electronic page make-up systems, colour transparencies are scanned in the traditional way on a drum scanner. The next stage is to feed the images into the system, then the operator manipulates and combines type, tint panels and pictures on screen following the designer's layout (above).

Colour proofs which have been generated electronically can be corrected conventionally – as to go back to the electronic system can be too expensive.

What are the different types of proofs?

THERE ARE NOW several types of colour proof available, but they can be divided into two types – wet proofs made on a proofing press and off-machine proofs.

WET PROOFS (also described as machine proofs) are achieved by making an aluminium printing plate from the separated film and printing it on a flat-bed proofing press, using the actual ink and paper which will be used on the final printed job.

The proofing press is actually a printing machine which is much slower than the press on which the job will finally be printed. The sheets of paper are fed by hand and the machine prints only one or two colours at a time rather than all four. It is not possible to produce more than a few dozen four-colour sheets an hour, compared with six or seven thousand on a printing press.

The advantage of wet proofing is that the designer can see something which is virtually identical to the final result and on the correct paper. Also, it has cost advantages where several proofs are required, as a proofing press can produce up to 24 sets of proofs economically, which is not possible with off-machine proofs.

The disadvantage is that it is more expensive and time-consuming when only one or two proofs are required, which is often the case. This is because a plate has to be made and this cannot be re-used for the actual printing if any corrections are necessary.

OFF-MACHINE PROOFS have been developed within the last ten years and use photographic rather than printing techniques. The two most common systems are Cromalin manufactured by Du Pont and Matchprint from 3M. In the Cromalin system, a sheet of white board is laminated with an ultra-violet light-sensitive laminate, the film is exposed onto it and the exposed image is then coloured with toner. The operation is repeated to achieve all four colours. A colour bar is included in the proof in order to check density, dot gain and grey balance.

In the Matchprint system, instead of using toner for the colours, a colour film is laminated to a sheet of white board, the film is exposed to it and then it is processed to give the first colour. This is repeated until all four colours have been built up on the board. Again a colour bar is incorporated.

COLOUR KEY is an earlier 3M system still in use, where four separate sheets of colour film are placed

Scatter proofs Also described as random proofs, this method of proofing is often used for books or simple magazines. They are cheaper than page proofs as they do not include type matter and so the pictures fit on far fewer sheets.

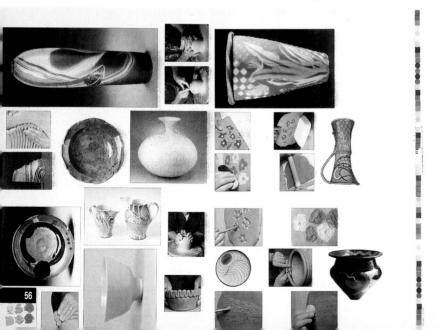

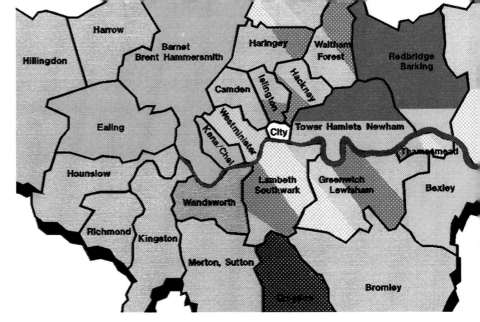

on top of each other and mounted on white paper. The colour achieved on this system is less accurate than that produced by Cromalin or Matchprint. All systems mentioned above are economical where only one or two proofs are required, but there is a problem in that the proofs have a higher dot gain than wet proofs or printing. This means that colours are more intense and the designer has to make allowance for this when checking colour.

SCATTER PROOFS to produce these the repro house scans the originals, masks them to size and imposes them to fit as many as possible on a proof sheet. Scatter proofs do not include type matter and are not laid out in the correct position relative to each other.

Scatter proofs can be the correct solution in two situations. First, where price is paramount and the job has only two or three pictures per page and a fairly straightforward layout. Here the colour can be approved and the repro house can send final film to the printer to do the page make-up, rather than have it done by the repro house. The designer would still see an imposed ozalid from the repro house to check positioning of pictures relative to type.

Scatter proofs are also used for a more complex job as a check on the colour quality before the repro house does make-up. This is more expensive as it involves two stages of proofing, but the cost can be justified when quality is paramount.

PAGE PROOFS show the type in position and include all tint panels etc. exactly as they will appear in the final job. They can be supplied as pairs of pages (double-page spreads) or imposed to the printer's imposition.

The advantage of imposed proofs is that the tracking (see page 141) can be checked, so that if one subject needs to carry a lot of magenta ink, for example, the designer can see what effect this will have on other subjects in the same track and make

the necessary adjustments before the printing stage.

The growth in popularity of electronic page make-up systems has made the use of page proofs much more common than previously.

FUTURE DEVELOPMENTS IN PROOFING include direct digital colour proofing (DDCP) in which the proofing system is linked directly to the scanner or page make-up system. The system takes the stored digital information, records it on an optical disk and outputs it through a digital writer onto the job paper, using liquid colours. The system is computer controlled, giving control of density, dot gain and other characteristics. The proof is identical to the finished printed result.

REMOTE MONITORS will become a common method of proofing in the future, particularly in high-volume magazine and advertising work. Here, the design studio will have a colour visual display unit linked to the repro house and this display can be checked both for colour and layout. Because the colour is not yet very accurate, this would be a "first proof", with the designer probably seeing a conventional form of proof before printing.

Thermal prints These are similar to DTP-produced laser proofs but in four colour. In terms of colour quality, they are no match for a proper proof. However, they offer a good visual reference to what the final printed piece will look like, and are useful for checking the position of elements before the repro house pushes the button for the colour proof run.

What are progressives?

When making wet proofs, the repro house will automatically make a set of progressive proofs at the same time as producing the four-colour proofs. Progressives show how the four-colour result is built up, one colour at a time. A set of progressives would therefore consist of 7 sheets. Each sheet is shown on this spread, though the sequence in which they are built up can vary from one repro house or printer to another.

Before four-colour printing presses were common, colour was printed one or two colours at a time and progressives were essential for the printer, to avoid putting too much or too little colour on the first three colours and only becoming aware of it when the last colour was printed. With the use of four-colour presses, progressives are less necessary.

When a designer is checking proofs, it can be helpful to also have the progressives, but only if the designer has the depth of technical knowledge to be able to make use of them. This very often involves also checking them with a densitometer (see page 75). In practice, however, most designers and clients do not check progressives, but on approval of proofs they are sent with the film to the printer.

It is not economical to make progressives using off-machine proofing methods such as Cromalin or Matchprint.

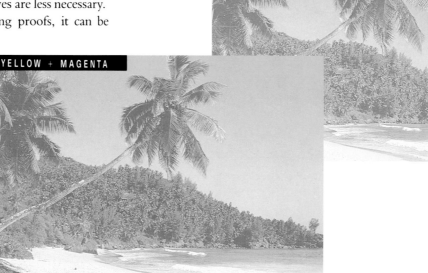

YELLOW

YELLOW + MAGENTA

MAGENTA

YELLOW + MAGENTA + CYAN

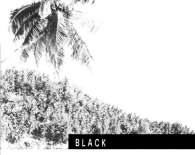

4-COLOUR

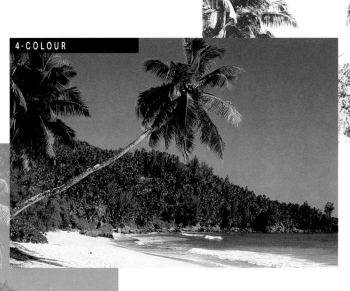

BLACK

CYAN

Progressive proofs These show how the final colour is built up. The films were proofed up in the correct printing sequence. The yellow is printed first, then the magenta, then the cyan, giving a three-colour process, and finally the black.

HOW DO I CHECK A PROGRESSIVE?

A great deal can be checked on progressives. At this stage it is best to use a densitometer to check ink weights and dot gains. The repro firm will read the densities and dot gains. You can also check the screen angles, and with some experience it is possible to tell a lot about each colour, check whether any shadows have filled in, and check that the highlights are printing in all colours, so as not to give any bias. You will need a linen tester to do this checking. Also check the actual colour of ink, as sometimes the proofs are not washed properly, resulting in inks dirtying the image.

Ultimately, the best check an inexperienced designer can make is to look at the four-colour proof only – progressives can be confusing to the untrained eye.

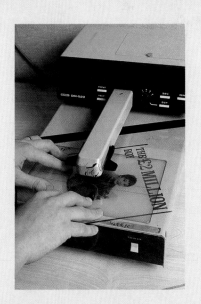

A variety of instruments are available for checking proofs; here a specialist densitometer is being used to ensure the film dot size is correct. Densitometers for proof checking are shown on

How does the repro house correct colour?

IF THE DESIGNER considers the colour proof not to be a good match to the original, the repro house can effect corrections as follows:

RESCANNING Here the repro house repeats the whole scanning procedure, but takes into account the corrections on the proof. The scanner can be adjusted to make any or all of the four colours stronger or weaker, improve definition and brightness, improve highlights or detail and many other characteristics. However, all these corrections must be done to the whole of the subject, as the scanner cannot deal with a specific area. Rescanning is the most common way of correcting colour.

MASKING Localized correction of the subject (for example, to make a face less red without reducing the red elsewhere in the picture) is done by masking off the area to be corrected and then contacting that area from negative to positive, varying exposure

CORRECTION COSTS

If a correction is required because of unsatisfactory work by the repro house, then there will be no charge. However, the repro house will obviously charge for any corrections which represent a change of mind by the designer or client. These corrections can be expensive and thus lead to possible conflict between designer and client or designer and repro house.

The safest course is to ensure that the client is shown detailed layouts or finished roughs and told of the financial penalties and possible time delay of changes of mind at proof stage.

On a scale of 1 to 10

Rescanning
10

Recropping bigger
8

Recropping smaller
7

Changing tint
4

Imposing a tint
4

Deletion
1

Moving type
1-5

reposition dot

delete type

strip-in new type

1320 Jews forced to wear a yellow badge

1028 Jews seized by pirates and ransomed to the Jews of Cairo and Alexandria

640 Heraclius ordered forcible conversions.
721 Leo III ordered baptism for all Jews and Muslims.
873 Basil I forbade practice of Judaism.
930 Romanos I encouraged baptism of Jews.

Line work To delete type (above), it is masked out on the black negative and a new, black final positive made. To strip in new type, it has to be shot, stripped into the black negative and contacted to a new final positive.

To reposition a bullet, which affects four colours, means remasking on the negatives for all four films and contacting four new final films.

Masking The vase (below) would need to be dry-dot etched to reduce all the colours. The retoucher makes a mask for the area of the vase and then contacts the colours to negative – with an increased exposure on the required area – before contacting them back to final positives.

Reduce all colours on vase

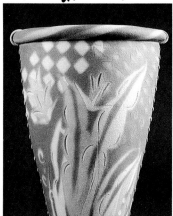

time to increase or decrease the size of the dot in the area to be altered. Increasing the dot size strengthens the colour and decreasing it weakens the colour. This technique is known as dry-dot etching.

HAND RETOUCHING is more expensive than the above two methods and most repro houses employ far fewer retouchers than were used in the past, as the improvements in scanners have resulted in less need for retouching.

Retouching is done using chemicals. The retoucher applies a staging lacquer to areas which are to remain unchanged, then applies chemicals to the film to reduce the size of the dots on the positive. If the dots have to be *increased* in size, then the retoucher works on a negative.

ELECTRONIC RETOUCHING On electronic page make-up systems, it is possible, though expensive, to correct the colour of the smallest area very accurately. This is because the system is capable of removing the dots of a colour in a particular area and replacing them with dots of any size. Taken to the extreme, the system can actually change the colour of a subject to a completely different colour. The high hourly cost rate of such systems means that they cannot economically be used for corrections which can easily be carried out by the above methods. Also, if the correction required is an author's correction, it may be worth getting a price before proceeding. The term "author's correction" is used to describe any correction for which the repro house can make an extra charge. It may be a change requested by the client, the copywriter or the designer.

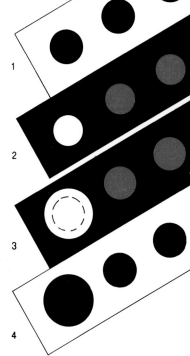

1

2

3

4

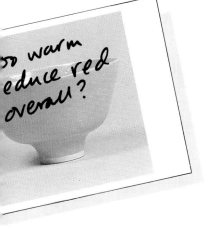

Hand retouching To reduce the magenta on the vase (above), the retoucher first applies an enamel paint to the positive to protect the dots in the background of the picture. The exposed area is then treated with chemicals, making the dots smaller on the vase only.

Electronic retouching To improve the contrast and detail in a specific area, it is best to retouch it on a system (below). First make a mask for the area required and then reduce the highlights and increase the shadows.

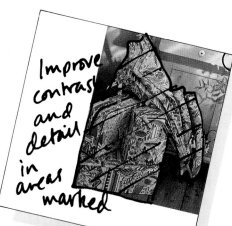

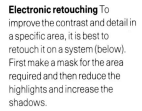

Rescan To increase colour and contrast overall on the vases, it is best to rescan (above).

To increase the dot The illustration above demonstrates diagrammatically the method used to increase the dot size when correcting colour.
1 Original film showing dot to be corrected. **2** The retoucher goes back to the negative film and masks off the (red) dots not to be worked on. **3** The unmasked dot is treated and made larger. **4** A new positive is made with the resulting larger dot.

To reduce the dot the retoucher would simply work on the positive, masking the dots to be left alone, and etching back the dot concerned.

What is dot gain?

THIS TERM describes the increase in the size of the dot caused by the processes that the image goes through between film and printing. The dot can grow at the following stages: platemaking (the exposed dot on the plate is bigger than the film dot); ink (tends to spread slightly beyond the dot area); printing on the blanket; blanket printing on the paper.

Other factors which affect the amount of dot gain include cylinder pressure, type of printing plate and type of printing machine (particularly if web- or sheet-fed, as web produces much more dot gain). The type of paper is also an important factor.

Dot gain is measured as the percentage by which the proofed or printed dot is larger than the original film dot. A wet proof has a dot gain of around 12% and off-machine proofs (for example, Cromalin) around 24%.

It would clearly be unacceptable for printed jobs to have stronger colours than originals or proofs, so the repro house has to ensure that the dot on the film is made artificially smaller than it should be. In this way the finished result is faithful to the original, despite dot gain.

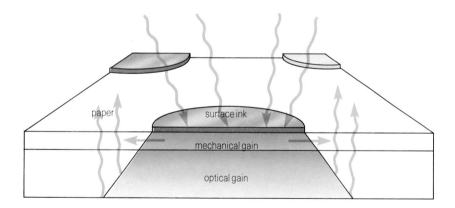

paper · surface ink · mechanical gain · optical gain

Cross-section through paper showing ink absorption Dot gain is a combination of mechanical gain (depending on ink, type of paper, plates and press which all influence the degree to which the ink sinks into the paper) and optical dot gain whereby the halftone dot on top of the paper gives a coloured shadow on the paper.

Dot gain tolerances The images (opposite) show various tolerances from the norm, in this case for the magenta film. These tolerances vary depending on cylinder pressure, age of rollers, temperature and so on, and demonstrate the variations which are acceptable in the mid-tones – that is, in the 50% dot. Obviously with highlight dots – which are normally about 3% – the tolerances are less, and the tolerances in the shadow area are less critical. Your origination house will have the spec sheet that tells them the dot gain factor of your printing and will adjust the dot to that dot gain, working within those tolerances.

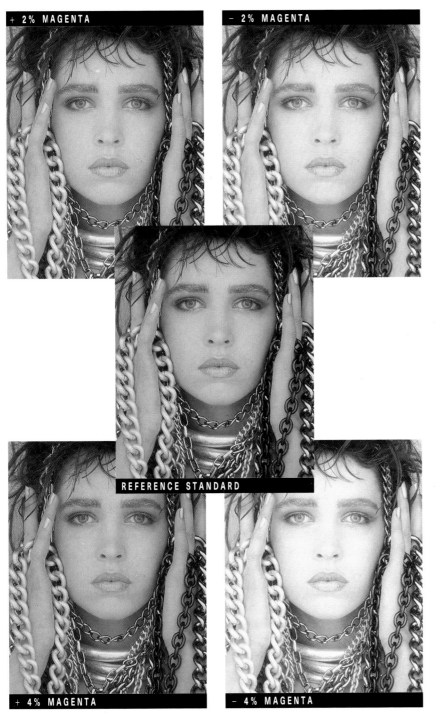

+ 2% MAGENTA

− 2% MAGENTA

REFERENCE STANDARD

+ 4% MAGENTA

− 4% MAGENTA

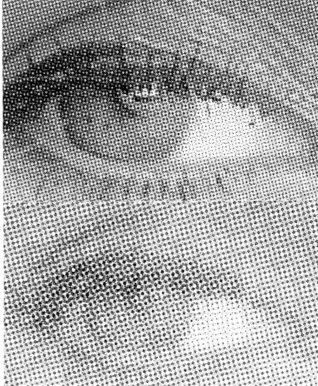

The effect of paper on dot gain
As these enlargements show an image reproduced on good-quality paper (top) shows the correct dot gain.
When it is reproduced on newsprint (above) the dots bleed into the paper.

What is moiré?

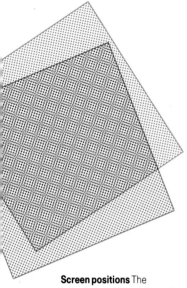

When a subject is printed, the dots of each colour are at a certain angle (see pages 72-73). If the dots of one colour are at the wrong angle, they will clash with the others, thus causing a moiré pattern. This happens most commonly on tints which are laid manually. It can also occur when two tints overlap.

Moiré patterning in four-colour sets is caused by something in the original interfering with the pattern of dots in the set. This often happens when a previously printed copy is scanned, and in this case the pattern of dots on the original clashes with the new pattern of dots on the scanned set.

Other subjects which can give rise to moiré include fabrics of fine dogtooth and Prince of Wales checks; tiling on roofs; photographs of pictures on TV screens; stereo loudspeakers. The repro house can alleviate the problem by reducing the detail, but this can affect the overall picture.

Screen positions The enlargement (above) shows the moiré effect caused when screens are positioned at the wrong angles. The two tints on the right will not clash when they are laid exactly on top of each other, at the correct angles.

Shoot dot for dot The moiré effect (right) is caused by having rescanned a previously printed image. The screen of the original separation is clashing with the screen of the new separation.

One solution (below) is to shoot the previously printed image dot for dot (on a camera not a scanner). This can only be done if the new separation is a similar size to the original. Otherwise the screen will be too coarse if enlarged and if reduced, too fine.

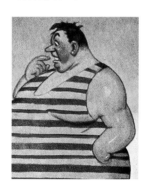

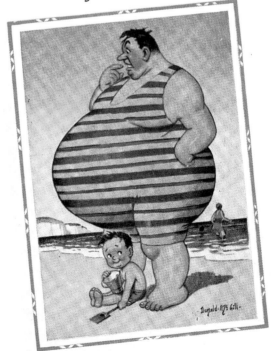

I CAN'T SEE MY LITTLE JOHNNY !

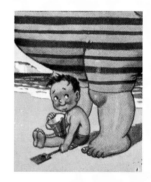

Soften dot Another solution is to put the original slightly out of focus, which makes the dots in the background merge into each other (above). However, this can result in some loss of detail.

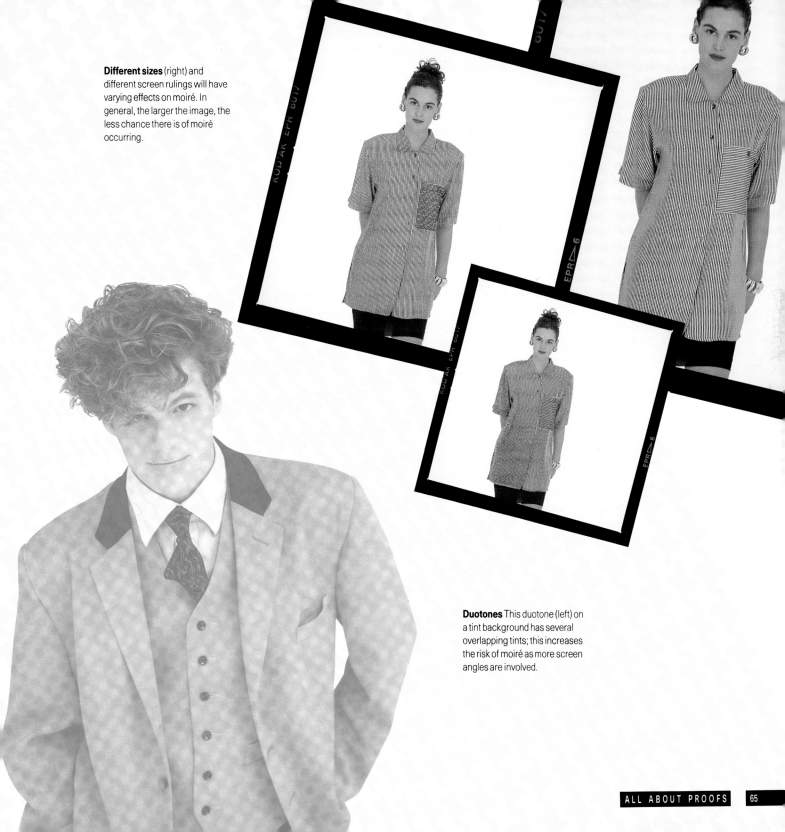

Different sizes (right) and different screen rulings will have varying effects on moiré. In general, the larger the image, the less chance there is of moiré occurring.

Duotones This duotone (left) on a tint background has several overlapping tints; this increases the risk of moiré as more screen angles are involved.

What are the industry standards?

As WELL AS the standards for viewing conditions for originals and proofs (see pages 74–75) and colour correction marks (see page 78), there are industry-wide standards for ink, colour bars and the specification of films and proofs supplied to printers.

INK for four-colour work. British printers work to British Standard 4666, which ensures that magenta, cyan and process yellow inks should be identical in colour at all repro houses and printers, even where the process inks are made by different manufacturers. Other countries' four-colour process inks differ slightly from the British standard and Japanese inks (which are also used in Hong Kong) in particular have stronger, brighter colours. In practice, most jobs can be proofed using British Standard inks and printed abroad using local standard inks without major problems. However, where quality is critical, the designer should ensure that the repro house obtains ink from the foreign printer for proofing.

The Pantone (PMS) colour-matching system for special colours is used throughout the world and is a reliable way of specifying special colours.

COLOUR BARS The most common control bars are shown here. The use of colour bars is described on page 70–71.

FIPP is the International Federation of the Periodical Press, which has issued the FIPP Specifications for European Offset Printing. The standards have been arrived at after discussions between publishers, repro houses and printers in most European countries and are widely accepted.

The need for some form of standardization arose from the fact that separations for magazines can come from many sources and to get good results on high-speed presses the originators of the film need to work to a common standard.

The standard includes specifications for artwork, film and proofs and, if applied correctly, would mean that an advertisement appearing in many magazines would always be consistently reproduced by different printers and in different magazines.

THE PANTONE SYSTEM

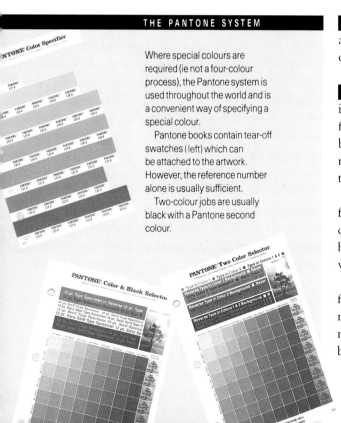

Where special colours are required (ie not a four-colour process), the Pantone system is used throughout the world and is a convenient way of specifying a special colour.

Pantone books contain tear-off swatches (left) which can be attached to the artwork. However, the reference number alone is usually sufficient.

Two-colour jobs are usually black with a Pantone second colour.

Colour bars There are various makes of colour bar. However, although they look different, they all share common elements (see page 70-71 for details). These are all for four-colour sheet-fed offset, but there are special colour bars available for 6-colour work and web-offset printing. Top to bottom:
Dupont Brunner Cromalin
GCA/GATF Proof Comparator II. The repro house makes a reference proof from the Proof Comparator films and sends it to the designer for subsequent referral. Thereafter all proofs that the colour house sends to the agency are accompanied by an image of the Proof Comparator. The designer then compares his or her reference image with the one on the proof.
GCA/GATF 85 line inch Colour Bar (used for newsprint, hence the coarser screen)
Gretag Matchprint
Gretag Wet Proof
Kinmei Printing Colour Bar (Japanese Printing Company).

At first glance these colour bars may all look very different. However, each bar contains the same basic elements.
1 Percentage screen patches.
2 Solid patches.
3 Coarse and fine screen patches.
4 Trapping patches.
5 Grey balance patch.
6 Highlight dot and microline patches.

The colour bars on this spread should not be used for any form of checking. They are reproduced here as examples for discussion only.

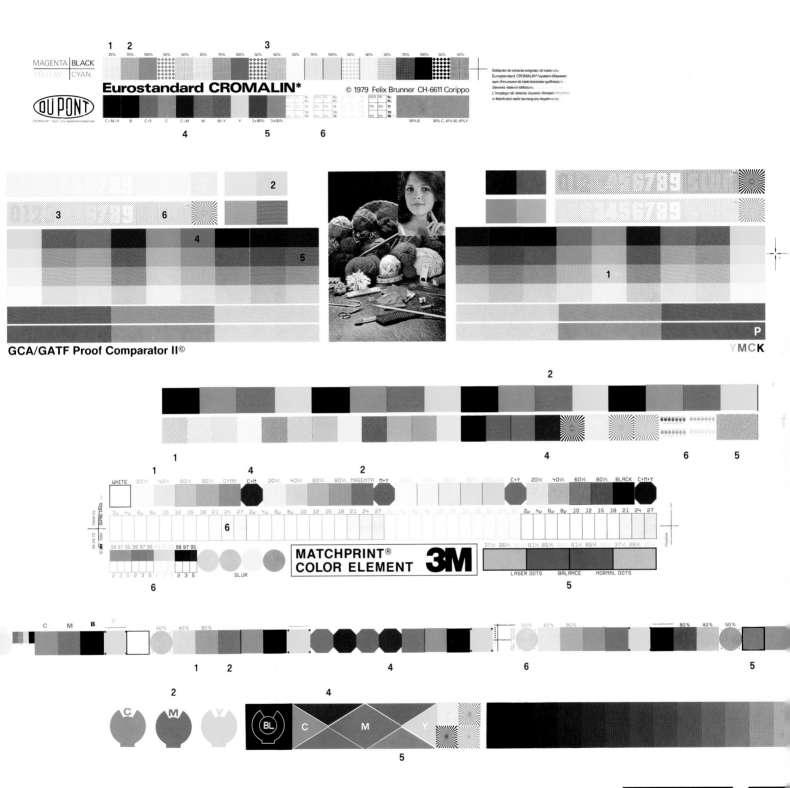

HOW TO CHECK

2

This section explains in detail what the designer should look for when checking proofs; the equipment required to do the job properly; how to mark up proofs and what colour bars are used for.

Examples are shown of proofs which are up or down in each of the four process colours or incorrect in other ways. Different subjects can present very different reproduction problems and examples of food, fashion, furniture, jewellery and other subjects are given, showing what can go wrong and how to correct it.

The section concludes with some repro house "nightmares".

How can colour bars help the designer check proofs?

On pages 66-67, you can see a range of international colour bars. Although they look different, they all measure the same characteristics and once you have learnt how to read one colour bar, you should be able to read all of them.

On this spread we look in detail at a Brunner colour bar.
1 25% and 75% screen patches.
2 Solid patches.
3 Coarse and fine screen patches.
4 Trapping patches.
5 Grey balance patch.
6 Highlight dot and microline patches.

The colour bar on this spread should not be used for any form of checking. It is reproduced here as an example for discussion only.

When film is prepared for proofing, a film of the colour bar (original, not duplicate film) is put on the edge of each piece of film. The colour bar then appears on the edge of the proof and can be checked for the characteristics shown here. The main point of using a colour bar is to check that the proof (and subsequently the printing) is carrying the correct weight of ink and that the plate (either the proofing plate or the printing plate) has been correctly exposed. If not, then it is difficult to check the colour

proof properly, since if the proofing process has applied too much or too little of a particular colour, the designer will find it difficult to check the separation. A colour bar is also essential for comparing dot gain (see pages 62-63).

Similarly, at the printing stage the printer will compare his colour bar with the one on the proof and if they are identical the printed result should be identical to the proof. If not, it means that the film of the subject is different from the proof, possibly due

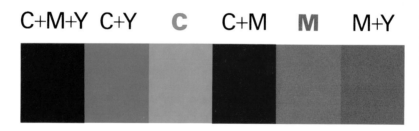

C+M+Y C+Y C C+M M M+Y

Trapping patches (left) Trapping happens when the first colour dries too much, which stops the following colours being absorbed into the paper. It gives a mottled effect, but can only be measured on a programmed densitometer.

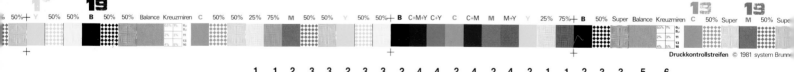

Druckkontrollstreifen © 1981 system Brunner

1 1 2 3 3 2 3 3 2 4 4 2 4 2 4 2 1 1 2 3 3 5 6

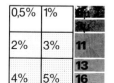

0,5%	1%	
2%	3%	11
		13
4%	5%	16

Plate
under exposed

0,5%	1%	6μ 8μ
2%	3%	11
		13
4%	5%	16

Accepted
Production
Tolerance

0,5%	1%	6μ 8μ
2%	3%	11
		13
4%	5%	16

Plate exposed
to meet
recommendation

0,5%	1%	6μ 8μ
2%	3%	11
		13
4%	5%	16

Accepted
Production
Tolerance

0,5%	1%	6μ 8μ
2%	3%	11
		13
4%	5%	16

Plate
over exposed

Positive plate exposure (left) These enable the printer and proofer to check that the plates have been exposed correctly. On an underexposed plate the dots are too heavy and on an overexposed plate they start to disappear.

to correction after proof stage.

As with progressives (see pages 58-59), the reading of colour bars is something most designers are not trained to do. Some therefore prefer to regard them as a tool for the repro house and printer. However, if you experiment with reading colour bars, you can gain a useful understanding.

Designers who know how to use a densitometer, check the colour bar to see if the proofing is correct. First, read the solid areas of each colour for the ink densities (see below) and then read the specified tint areas to check the dot gain. If one of the colours has been proofed with either the wrong dot gain or density, it will affect the neutral grey areas on the colour bar and this will help you to identify which colour is incorrect. Grey balance is 50% dot on cyan and 38% to 40% on magenta and yellow.

Manufacturers of densitometers use slightly different filters in the instrument's reading head and the readings can differ according to whether narrow- or broad-band filters are used. The designer should check the comparison chart that is normally supplied by the manufacturer.

DENSITY is the light-stopping or light-absorbing ability of an object and is measured in printing on a logarithmic scale ranging from 0.0 to 3.0. It is measured with a densitometer.

Printers set up their presses to their own standards, which are set out in the printer's specification (see page 32). Smaller presses have smaller inking rollers, which exert less pressure and are therefore not capable of carrying the same weight of ink as bigger presses. With a small press the printer will use slightly lower ink densities.

Checking plate exposure
(below) A visual guide for the platemaker for checking plate exposure. If the crosses within the circles disappear then there is something wrong with the plate exposure.

50% 50%

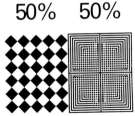

Dot gain (right) The coarse screen 50% gives you an at-a-glance check on dot gain. The fine screen can be read with a densitometer programmed with the Murray Davies equation, which gives the exact amount of dot gain. These are shown (left) enlarged.

Super

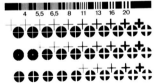

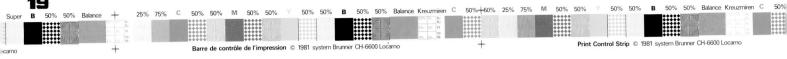

Balance (left) This enables you to see immediately whether all the colours are proofed in balance. When proofed correctly, it should appear as a neutral grey.

Balance

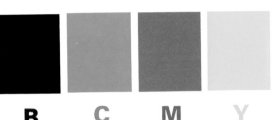

Density (left) The individual solid colours (cyan, magenta, yellow and black) are for reading the ink densities, which should match the printer's specifications.

B C M Y

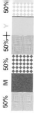

How do I check screen ruling and angles?

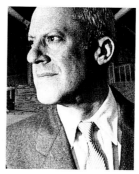
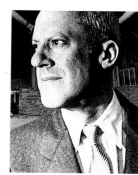

DIFFERENT COLOURS have different screen angles and if the angles are not correct then moiré patterning can result (see pages 64-65). Normally, the repro house has the scanner set up properly, so the designer need not check the screen angles on every proof, but only if there is a problem such as moiré.

Screen testers To check the screen angles, keep the bottom edge of the tester square to the bottom of the picture, and a circle will appear around a line on the tester. For example, on the magenta it will appear around 45%. To check the screen ruling, lay the tester on the film and turn it until a star shape appears with one corner pointing to the screen number. Your repro house will supply you with both testers as they are part of its standard equipment. However, the designer can lose nothing by knowing how to use a tester.

Most UK repro houses use imperial screen rulings (for example, 85, 100, 133, 150).

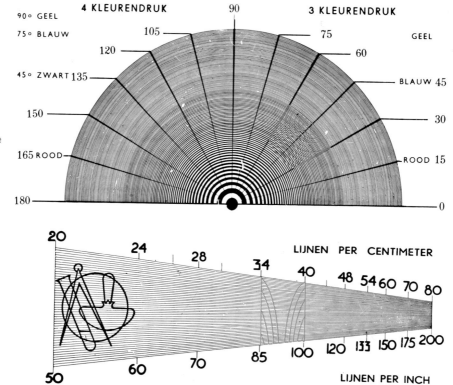

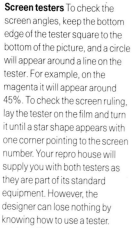

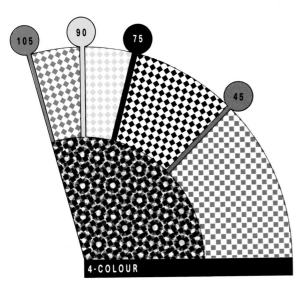

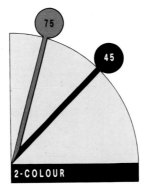

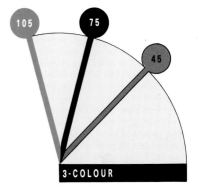

Halftone screens These are placed at an angle of 45° (opposite page, top right) so that the pattern of dots produced is not visible to the eye. Compare with the 90° screen (opposite page, top left).

Checking angles It is important to make sure that all colours are at the correct angles, otherwise moiré patterning can occur. In four-colour printing (above) the magenta is at 45°; the cyan is 105° (this can also be called 15° – they are the same); the black is 75°; the yellow is 90°.

Checking two-colour angles The lightest colour is on the most prominent angle – 75°, and the black on 45°.

Checking three-colour angles This is the same as two-colour, but the third colour is angled at 105° (15°).

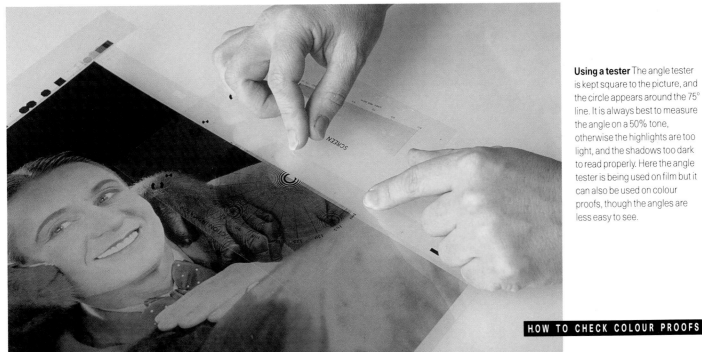

Using a tester The angle tester is kept square to the picture, and the circle appears around the 75° line. It is always best to measure the angle on a 50% tone, otherwise the highlights are too light, and the shadows too dark to read properly. Here the angle tester is being used on film but it can also be used on colour proofs, though the angles are less easy to see.

What equipment do I need to check proofs?

To check proofs properly, you will need certain equipment. The items described below make the job easier and the designer more efficient.

TRANSPARENCY VIEWER (lightbox) These are available in various sizes, but what is more important is that the lighting conforms to the national standard (in Britain this is BS 950). This standard defines the colour and intensity of the light source and is the one to which most transparency viewers used at repro houses and printers conform. This means that the transparency is viewed under the same lighting conditions at the various stages of reproduction and printing. Ensure that the tubes are replaced at the recommended intervals.

VIEWING BOOTH Although bulkier than transparency viewers, viewing booths can be obtained in sizes as small as A3, small enough to fit into the most crowded studio. They are used to view the proofs and flat artwork. The lighting in the viewing booth should conform to the national standard (BS 950 in Britain).

SCREEN-ANGLE TESTER The different process colours have different screen angles (see pages 72-73) and the tester consists of a piece of film. Your repro house will probably be able to let you have one free of charge.

SCREEN TESTER This tests the screen ruling. Like the screen-angle tester, it consists of a piece of film

and should be obtainable from your repro house.

LINEN TESTER This is the type of magnifying glass used by repro houses and printers to view 35mm colour transparencies. The folding stand means that the lens is the correct distance from the subject and the hands are left free. The linen tester is used to view both transparencies and colour proofs.

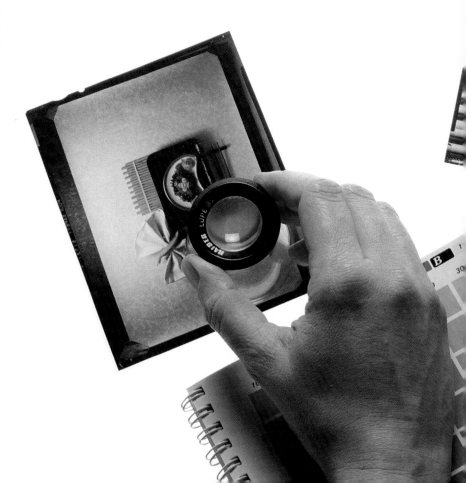

A 35mm transparency (below) is difficult to view and needs to be magnified to check detail areas. The naked eye is usually sufficient to check colour proofs, and magnification with a linen tester is usually only needed to check register or damaged film.

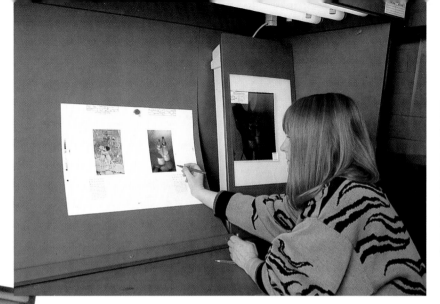

Most designers have transparency viewers, but very few have viewing booths (left) despite the fact that they are essential for proper colour correction. Without a viewing booth, the colours of the proof will be affected by both the type of lighting in use in the studio and outside weather conditions. This makes it very difficult to correct colour accurately.

DO I NEED A DENSITOMETER?

A densitometer (right) is a sophisticated and expensive electronic device used to check the density of ink on a proof by reading the colour bars (see pages 66-67). It cannot be used without a deeper technical knowledge than is required of most designers, and is not essential.

Repro houses and printers use it to compare the densities of proofs, film, colour bars and the final printed result.

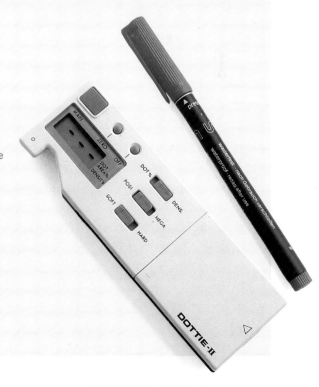

What are the basic elements to check?

Backgrounds of tints or special colours If a common special colour or tint background is required for several pages in a publication, the designer should be aware of problems the printer might have in maintaining consistency between pages.

For example, if a buff background is used, consisting of a percentage tint of process yellow, and there are some pages which require a heavy weight of yellow to be run for the pictures, the tints on those pages will be heavier than on the other pages. The use of a special fifth colour (a Pantone colour, for example) for the backgrounds only, should avoid this problem. But remember that it is more expensive to run five colours than four.

Colour bar This tells the designer whether the proof is faithful to the film being proofed. For example, if the proofer has used too much yellow ink, so that the proof looks too yellow even though the film is correct, the colour bar will show this.

If a proof is bad either because the colour is way out, or because the layout, sizing or position has been done incorrectly, there may be a case for rejecting it without the client or designer checking it, on the grounds that the client would be so disappointed that he would lose confidence in the designer or repro house. However, even though a proof may not be shown to the client, it is usually worth the designer checking it, as there may be a design error as well as the repro house's mistake, and changing it at this stage saves a further proof later.

Rejection can also occur when the client and designer insist on a reproof because the checked proof is so different from the original that the designer, without seeing a reproof, cannot be confident that correction will be carried out properly.

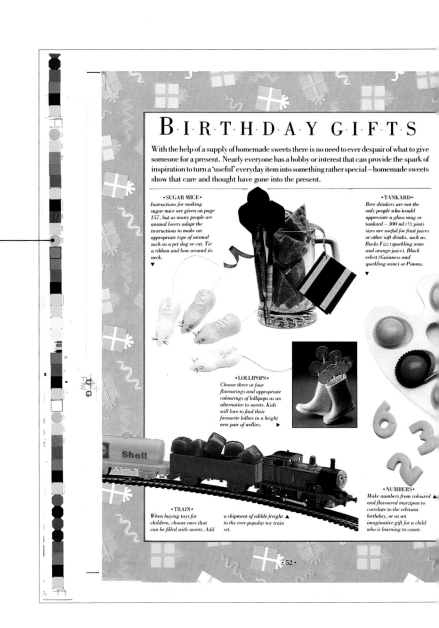

B·I·R·T·H·D·A·Y G·I·F·T·S

With the help of a supply of homemade sweets there is no need to ever despair of what to give someone for a present. Nearly everyone has a hobby or interest that can provide the spark of inspiration to turn a 'useful' everyday item into something rather special – homemade sweets show that care and thought have gone into the present.

·SUGAR MICE·
Instructions for making sugar mice are given on page 157, but as many people are animal lovers adapt the instructions to make an appropriate type of animal such as a pet dog or cat. Tie a ribbon and bow around its neck.

·TANKARD·
Beer drinkers are not the only people who would appreciate a glass mug or tankard – 300 ml (½ pint) sizes are useful for fruit juices or other soft drinks, such as, Bucks Fizz (sparkling wine and orange juice), Black velvet (Guinness and sparkling wine) or Pimms.

·LOLLIPOPS·
Choose three or four flavourings and appropriate colourings of lollipops as an alternative to sweets. Kids will love to find their favourite lollies in a bright new pair of wellies.

·TRAIN·
When buying toys for children, choose ones that can be filled with sweets. Add a shipment of edible freight ▲ to the ever-popular toy train set.

·NUMBERS·
Make numbers from coloured ▲ and flavoured marzipan to correlate to the relevant birthday, or as an imaginative gift for a child who is learning to count.

· 52 ·

Mechanical tints When first specifying the tint, always give percentages of the process colours, which can be obtained from a tint chart, rather than giving a Pantone colour swatch or reference number to match, as many special colours cannot be obtained from the four-colour process. The tint on the proof can then be checked against the tint chart. Watch out for mottled tints, which can be caused by the film or plate being exposed out of contact. Look also for moiré.

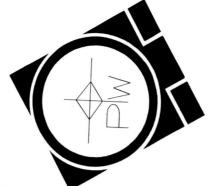

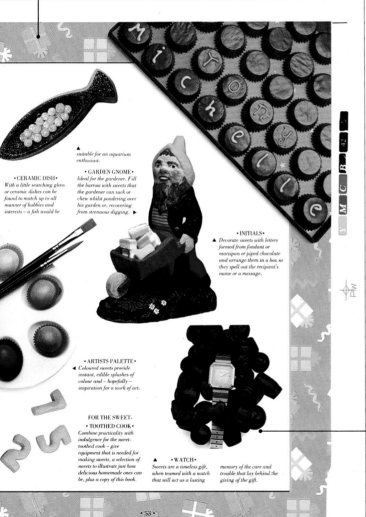

Register Check registration marks to see if the job has been proofed in register. If it is correct, all you will see is black. If it is out of register, one or more colours will show next to the black.

Trim and bleed Check trim marks for position and that the bleed allowance is correct.

"Flopping" When a picture appears reversed left to right in a colour proof, it should be marked "flop". This correction is not simply a matter of the repro house turning the film over, as the emulsion would be on the wrong side and therefore out of contact with the plate. Instead, a new contact film has to be made so that the emulsion is on the right side.

Fit If the register marks fit, but you can see colours sticking out from the edge of the picture (right), the job has been planned out of fit.

Always check the following:

1 Register

2 Trim and bleed

3 Sizes – if a grid is used, check proof against it

4 Type – broken, missing, illegible, too fine

5 Colour – check the colour bar

6 Flopped subjects

7 Artwork overlays

8 Tints

9 Special colours

10 Returns – check repro house has sent back all artwork and colour transparencies originally supplied.

11 Gutter

PROOF CORRECTION

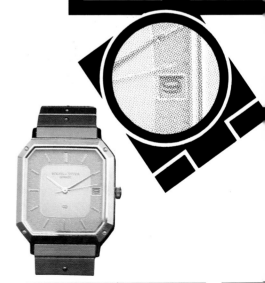

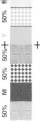

What are the rules for marking up proofs?

THE ANSWER to this question depends to a large extent on how much technical knowledge the designer has. The following pages look specifically at checking size, crop, position etc., but it is the way the designer marks up colour corrections that is crucial to a successful finished result.

If the designer does not have in-depth technical knowledge of reproduction, it is much better to state the result required, rather than tell the repro house how to achieve it. For example, if the proof has an area of green which is lighter than the green on the transparency, the instruction "Make this green darker – see original" is sufficient to tell the repro house what needs doing. Telling the repro house *how* to do the correction would involve saying "increase cyan", possibly even mentioning by what percentage the cyan should be increased. However, colour correction is an area where a little knowledge is a dangerous thing. In the example above, the designer may not know enough to realize that the cyan strength is correct, but it is the yellow that needs to be reduced.

For most designers then, the correction of colour consists in marking up the proofs where the colour is not sufficiently close to the original and saying in what way it differs. It is not enough to say "Reproof – see original"; you must indicate to the repro house in what way you think the proof differs.

The designer should not write a little essay about the proof, such as "The trees look a rather darker green than the transparency, but the blue in the river should not be any lighter and the sky is correct", but specify "Lighten green in trees". If a proof is nearly correct, it is best to accept it, as to request correction and a reproof may result in over-correction.

Where a reproof is required, this should be stated clearly. Knowing when to ask for reproofs is a matter of experience, but as a general rule, if the proof is so far away from the original that you are worried that it may still not be correct after correction, then a reproof is justified.

STANDARD COLOUR CORRECTION MARKS

The symbols in British Standard BS 4785 are not often used, but can be useful if the designer has the technical knowledge to mark up proofs in this way. It probably involves knowing how to use a densitometer, and how to read colour bars.

The instruction "improve detail and modelling" refers to the highlights and details that need enhancing. Hardness and softness are the terms used to describe whether the edges of a colour, shape or tone are either too sharp or too indistinct.

If an image is out of register, the films for one or more of the four colours have been misaligned. If the edges of the image are not in register, the film has been positioned incorrectly on the plate. "Slur" refers to a proofing defect which elongates the halftone dots.

Instruction	Marginal mark
1 Passed for press	
2 Reproof	
3 Reduce contrast	
4 Increase contrast	
5 Improve detail or modelling	
6 Too hard, make softer	U
7 Too soft, make sharper	∧
8 Rectify uneven tint	
9 Repair broken type, rule or tint	X
10 Improve register	
11 Correct slur	

Process colour	Increase	Reduce
Yellow	Y+	Y−
Magenta	M+	M−
Cyan	C+	C−
Black	B+	B−

CORRECT

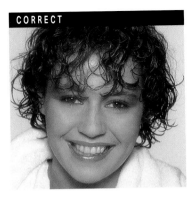

TOO MUCH CONTRAST

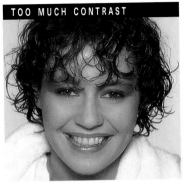

TOO LITTLE CONTRAST

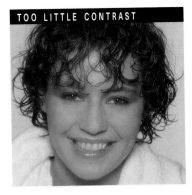

This gives some idea of how many different faults a proof can have. The errors in all these pictures are only slight, but the slightest difference can change a picture entirely. All of these faults are described in more detail later.

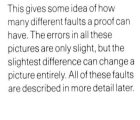

LOSS OF DETAIL

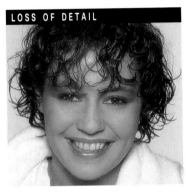

DETAIL TOO HARD

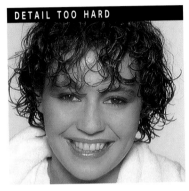

DETAIL TOO SOFT

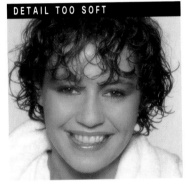

TOO MUCH CYAN

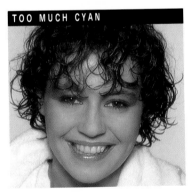

TOO MUCH MAGENTA

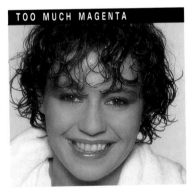

TOO MUCH YELLOW

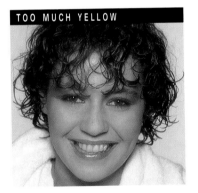

TOO LITTLE CYAN

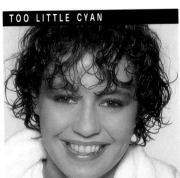

TOO LITTLE MAGENTA

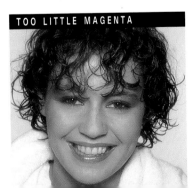

TOO LITTLE YELLOW

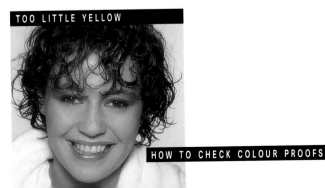

How should I go about making my marks?

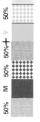

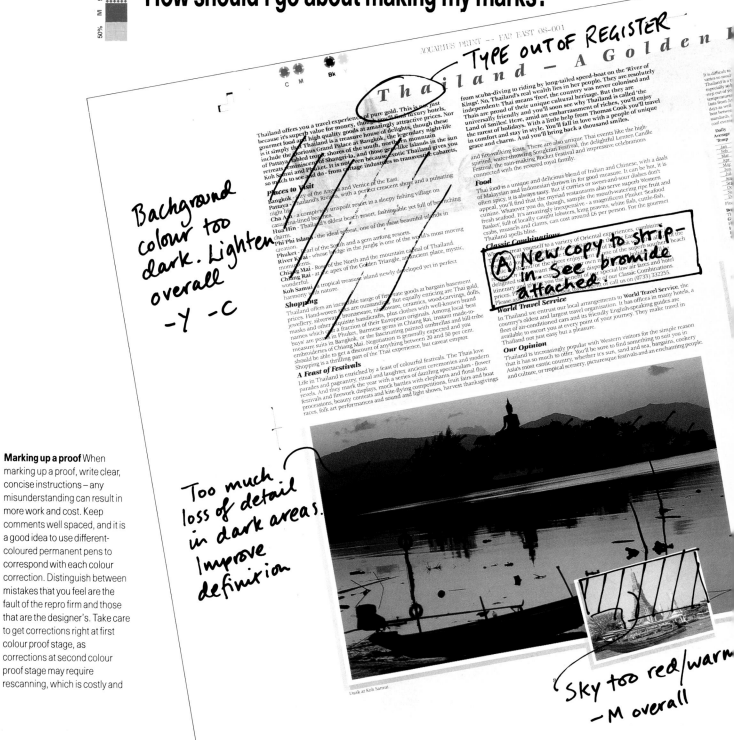

Marking up a proof When marking up a proof, write clear, concise instructions – any misunderstanding can result in more work and cost. Keep comments well spaced, and it is a good idea to use different-coloured permanent pens to correspond with each colour correction. Distinguish between mistakes that you feel are the fault of the repro firm and those that are the designer's. Take care to get corrections right at first colour proof stage, as corrections at second colour proof stage may require rescanning, which is costly and time-consuming. It is not always necessary for a reproof to be proofed in the same way as the first proof. For example, the first proof may be a wet proof of which several sets have been done, but a Cromalin may suffice for the reproof and will be cheaper. If the change concerns only size or position and not colour, then the reproof can be an ozalid.

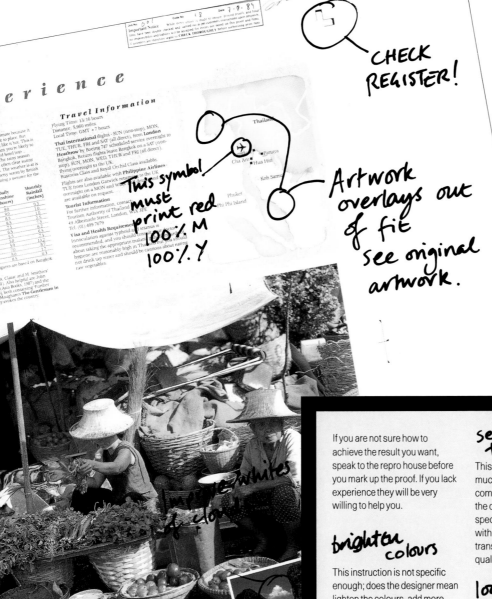

AVOIDING AMBIGUOUS INSTRUCTIONS

If you are not sure how to achieve the result you want, speak to the repro house before you mark up the proof. If you lack experience they will be very willing to help you.

brighten colours

This instruction is not specific enough; does the designer mean lighten the colours, add more colour or improve contrast?

— improve magenta

If the designer gives this instruction on a colour proof the repro house is left wondering whether the instruction is to minus magenta or improve magenta. The ambiguity lies in the fact that a handwritten minus sign can be mistaken for a dash.

see transparency

This type of instruction is not so much ambiguous as non-committal. As much as possible, the designer should always specify what is actually *wrong* with the proof. To say "See transparency" without any qualifications is simply sloppy.

looks too warm

Does the designer mean the proof looks too magenta or too yellow?

make greener

What colour green is greener? With this instruction does the designer mean emerald green, pea green, lime green, sage green, bottle green; leaf green...? This type of ambiguity can occur with any colour.

improve quality

Another woolly instruction which will have the repro house wondering what the designer means – is the instruction referring to the films not matching, the colour density not being right or one or all of the colours being overdone?

you haven't caught the mood of this shot

An instruction guaranteed to irritate. The scanner operator does not have a "mood" button. The operator will have matched the transparency unless a specific other instruction was given on the layout.

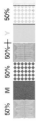

What is a good black and white halftone?

A GOOD BLACK AND WHITE original should be sharp and have reasonable contrast. Although the repro house can increase contrast, it is always easier to start with an original with a good density range. When reproduced, a good black and white original will have a pin dot in the highlight areas and just stay open enough in the shadows to hold detail, while being heavy enough to make a good strong black.

With a bad black and white reproduction, the proof could either show the highlight dot as too large, making the picture look flat, or too small, making the whites blown out and coarse. If it is the shadow areas which are wrong, it will be because either the shadow setting is too low, resulting in the shadow areas being too light and grey, or because it is too high, so that filling in and loss of detail occur.

This picture has too much contrast and has lost detail. The highlights have dropped out, losing the detail on the tie, the shadows have filled in, resulting in loss of texture on the jacket.

This picture is too flat, the whites look grey, and the shadows are grey instead of black. The overall effect is insipid.

A good black and white picture should be sharp, crisp and punchy (left). There should be a very small dot on the highlights for detail, but it should carry enough weight to look black. Using a glass (below) to look at the good halftones reveals that the contrast is set correctly with good white highlights appearing on the watch.

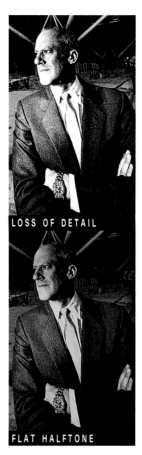

LOSS OF DETAIL

FLAT HALFTONE

GOOD BLACK AND WHITE HALFTONE

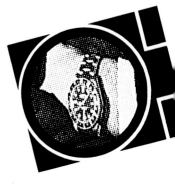

What is good black and white line repro?

If you want to give a coloured effect to the picture, you can add a flat tint such as yellow to give the effect of antique paper (below).

A GOOD black and white line original should have clean, strong areas of black. Where the lines are very fine or broken, the original may have to be treated as a halftone or a line and tone combination. This is often the case with old line engravings, where the lines are so fine and close together that line reproduction will lose detail by making the darker areas solid.

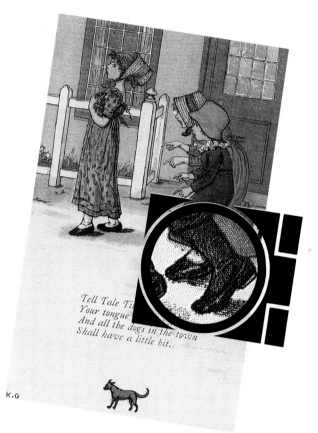

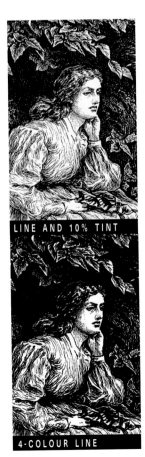

LINE AND 10% TINT

4-COLOUR LINE

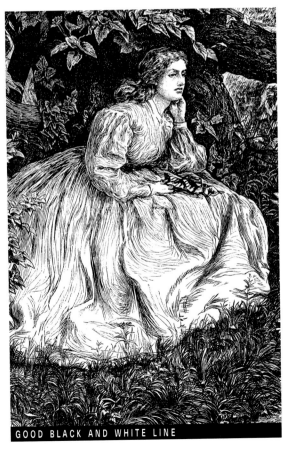

GOOD BLACK AND WHITE LINE

With a good black and white line shot (left), you should check that the shadows have not filled in and that the very fine lines in the highlights are printing. If either of these is wrong, ask the repro house to re-shoot them. It is very difficult to reproduce these line shots as four-colour, as the tones are so thin that it is nearly impossible to register the colours exactly (far left).

With some pictures, especially those with type, it is possible to shoot the three colours (cyan, magenta and yellow) conventionally, then to shoot a line of the black, which is combined with the normal black tone. It gives greater definition to the picture and type, but check the price with the repro house first, as it is likely to be expensive. This postcard (above) was proofed with a combination of tone and black line.

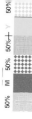

What is a good duotone?

It is a mistake for a designer to think that a poor black and white original can be improved by reproducing it as a duotone, as all it will make is a poor duotone.

A true duotone is produced when two halftone films of the same subject are printed in different colours. The heavier colour (usually black) has a 45° screen angle and is reproduced to full range, with dots from 5% to 95%. The second, lighter colour is at a different angle and is usually heavier in the highlights, with a range of 15% to 95%. The designer may not want the full range of the lighter colour and could ask for it to print at only 60% strength, giving a range of 2% to 60%. This can be difficult to visualize and the designer should discuss it with the repro house and look at examples of similar previous jobs.

With some high-quality black and white work, such as photography books, duotones are reproduced so as to look like black and whites and use a very pale grey as the second colour. This can give very good results. The grey brings out the midtones – giving more body to the printed piece.

Another way to reproduce a black and white picture in two colours is to print a black and white halftone in black on a percentage tint panel of a second colour. This is sometimes wrongly described as a duotone. It will result in less depth and detail than a true duotone.

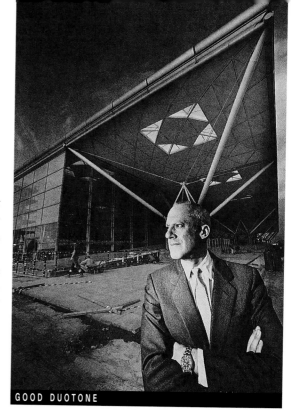

GOOD DUOTONE

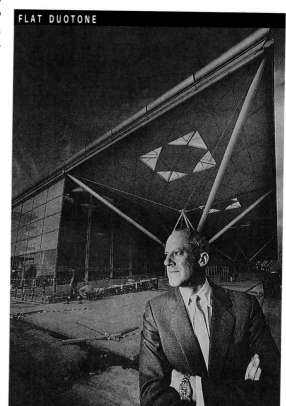

FLAT DUOTONE

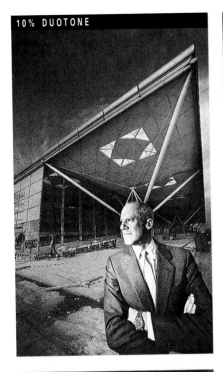

10% DUOTONE

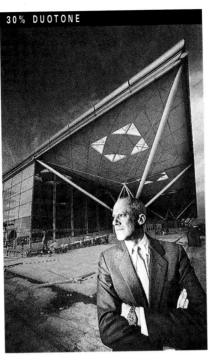

30% DUOTONE

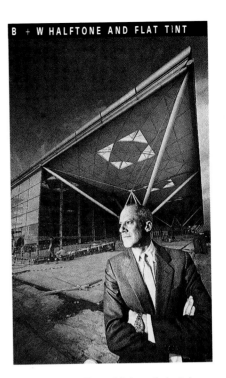

B + W HALFTONE AND FLAT TINT

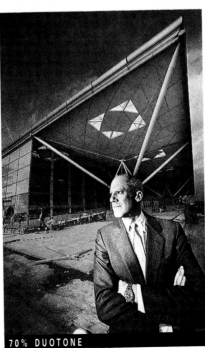

50% DUOTONE

70% DUOTONE

The pictures on this spread show some of the different effects you can achieve with duotones. On the opposite page, the top image is full strength, while the bottom one looks flat and uninteresting. The block of four shown left show different strengths of the cyan from the very subtle 10%, which gives just a touch of blue to the highlights, to three-quarters strength. The halftone with a flat cyan tint (above) looks flat compared with the real thing.

The moiré picture (below) shows what can happen when both colours are at the same screen angle.

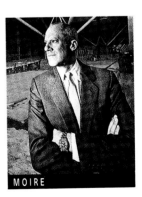

MOIRE

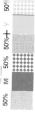

What is a good four-colour black/sepia?

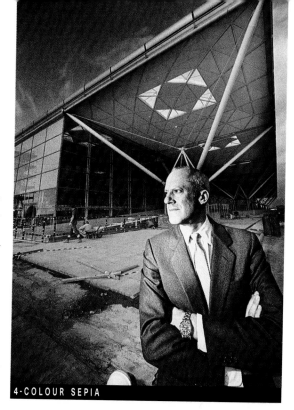

4-COLOUR SEPIA

With the use of scanners making the practice more economic, a lot of designers now use four-colour black and whites. These give a very strong black and good detail. They also allow very subtle shades of colour to come through, instead of just grey, black or white.

The originals are scanned just as if they were colour originals and it is possible to run a particular colour stronger to give, for example, a red tinge to a black and white photo, although this will need to be discussed with the repro house. The balance of the colours depends on the requirements of the designer.

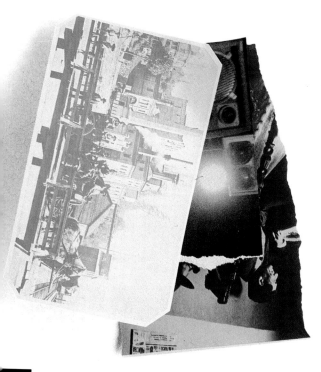

3-COLOUR SEPIA

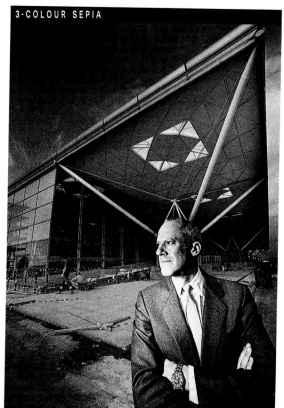

Sepia effects Sepias come in many different shades, so for the best result always supply the repro house with a tear-sheet of the result you require (left). Tear-sheets can be taken from magazines and publications. A three-colour sepia effect can look as effective as a four-colour version, and the former is cheaper to print (right top and bottom).

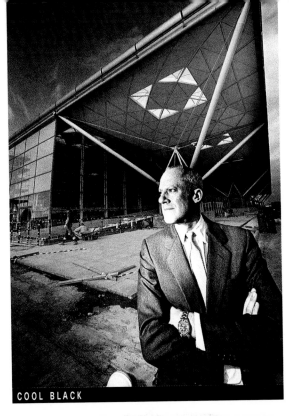

COOL BLACK

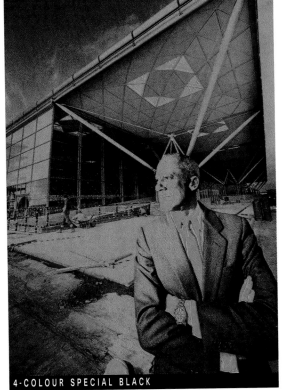

4-COLOUR SPECIAL BLACK

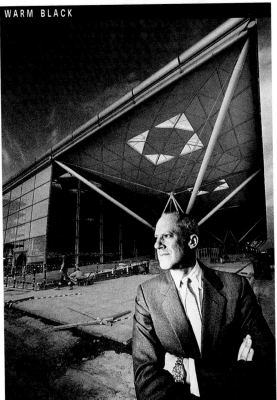

WARM BLACK

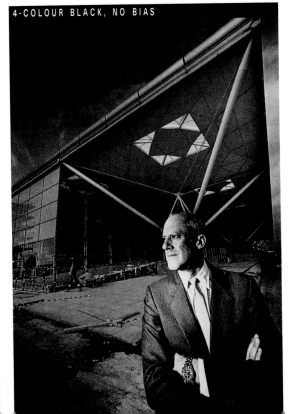

4-COLOUR BLACK, NO BIAS

In the first picture (far left) the cyan is slightly above the magenta and yellow, giving a cool effect. This seems to work well with pictures of machinery, giving a modern look. The warm picture (below left) has the magenta as the predominant colour, giving a sepia-like effect. The neutral picture (below right) has all the colours in the correct balance, but allows subtle shades to come through. In the special effect (above right) the magenta is printed in negative, giving pink highlights and greenish shadows.

Remember that although the repro house can reproduce a colour transparency to print as black and white, it cannot convert a colour transparency to four-colour black, as the scanner can only reproduce it as full colour. The solution is to make a black and white print from the transparency and reproduce it as four-colour black.

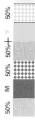

How do I know if the proof is too flat?

If the job looks flat overall, this can be caused either by the highlight dots being set too big or by the dot in the shadow being set too small (right). If the highlight dots are too big, the whites will appear slightly grey. If the shadow dots are too small, the black will not come out strong enough, and all the shadows will need to be increased.

If the proof lacks punch and none of the colours seem bright enough, then the shadows are too open and they and the midtones should be increased.

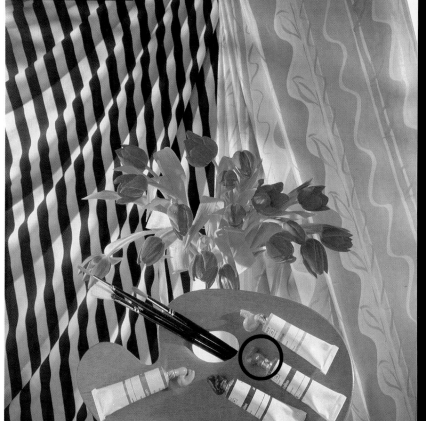

FLAT PROOF

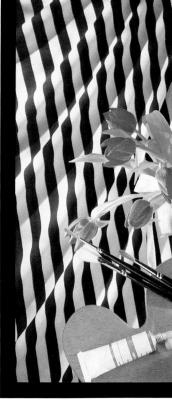

FINAL PROOF

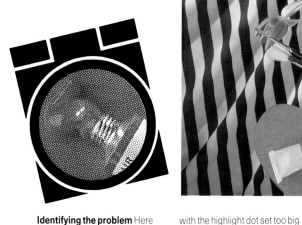

Identifying the problem Here you can see a large dot of cyan on the reds, making the picture dirty (above). To be correct, the cyan dot should be as fine as possible. The proof is too flat and has been scanned incorrectly, with the highlight dot set too big and the shadow dot set too small. To correct the picture, it will have to be rescanned. Compared with the final proof (centre), the highlights are grey instead of white, all the colours look dirty, and the shadows are grey instead of black.

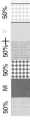

How do I know if the proof is too weak?

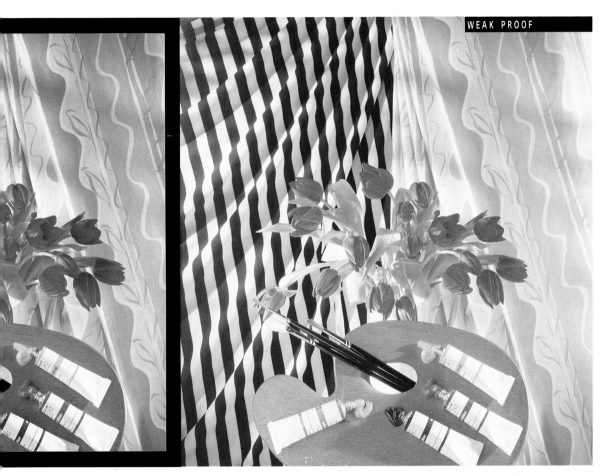

WEAK PROOF

To check whether the proof is too weak have a look at all the tints on the job. If these are too light, it is likely that the proof has been run with too little ink on one or more colours. The colour sets will look thin and the black shadow areas will appear slightly grey, with the midtones also thin (left).

If the tints are correct but the colour sets look thin, they may have been scanned incorrectly. If you do not have a densitometer, ask the repro house to read the ink densities and mark them on the proof.

Checking the colour bar
Viewed through a linen tester, the colour bar shows a weak proof of the 40% dot of the cyan, which is only half strength (right). The 80% is also below strength. This tells you that the film is correct, but the proof has been run with too little cyan.

This proof (above) is weak. The fault lies either with the proofing or the scanning, and checking the colour bar will tell you which is at fault. Here, the scanning is incorrect, with the highlight dots and shadow dots both set too small. The whites on the paint tubes have lost all the detail, the shadows look grey rather than black, and all the colours look very pale.

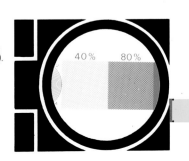

40%   80%

How do I know if the highlights are poor?

Here, the highlight dots have been set too small on scanning, which has caused a loss of detail in the lighter areas (right). As a result, all the pastel colours look thin.

This has also affected the complementary colours that give modelling, such as the cyan on the red flowers which lack definition and shape. It is not caused by proofing, as that would not affect the smaller dots to such an extent.

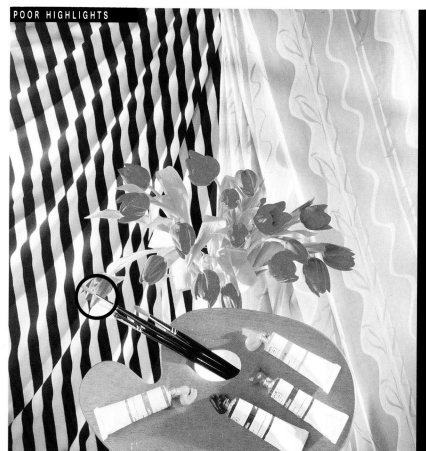

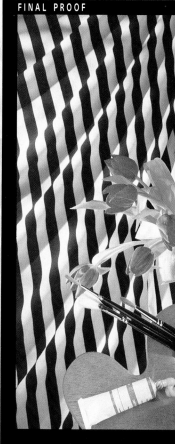

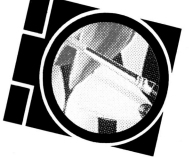

Identifying the problem
Looking at part of the proof through a linen tester shows that the highlight dots are too small. If they were increased, they would stand out from the white paper areas giving more definition in the highlights. The darker reds should have a small cyan dot for modelling, also.

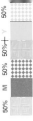

How do I know if the proof is too dense?

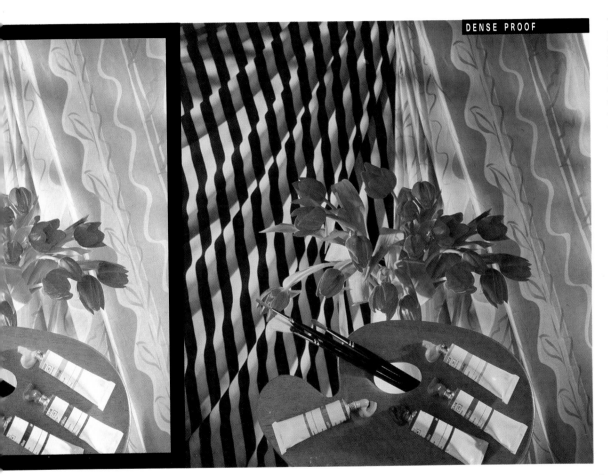

DENSE PROOF

This proof is too dense (left). If it is caused by the ink, the 40% and 80% steps will have filled in. If these are correct, it is a fault in reproduction. Here, all the colours look too strong: the red flowers have gone brown, the yellows are orange, and the whites look grey.

Checking the colour bar If the proof carries too much ink, the three-colour neutral will look too dark – nearly black instead of dark grey.

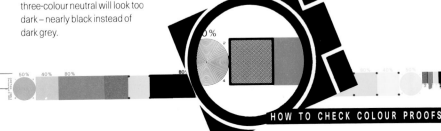

How do I know if the proof is up or down on cyan?

If a proof is up on the cyan, the three-colour grey will have a blue cast. To see if this is caused by the magenta and yellow being down, check the 40% and 80% cyan steps on the colour bar. If they have filled in, the proof is up on cyan. If these are correct, the fault is in the reproduction.

Here, the whites and greys have a blue cast, the yellows look green, the pinks in the curtain are too dirty, and the red flowers are going brown.

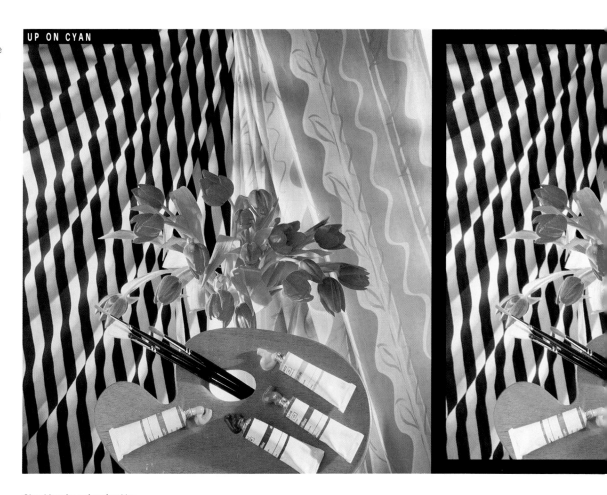

UP ON CYAN

Checking the colour bar You can see that the cyan 80% step has filled in and looks the same as the 100% step next to it. This shows that the proof has too much cyan ink.

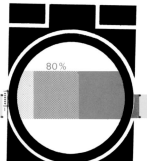

80%

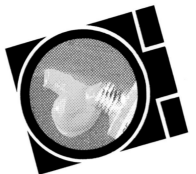

Identifying the problem When a proof is down on cyan, there is virtually no cyan dot in the enlarged area (left).

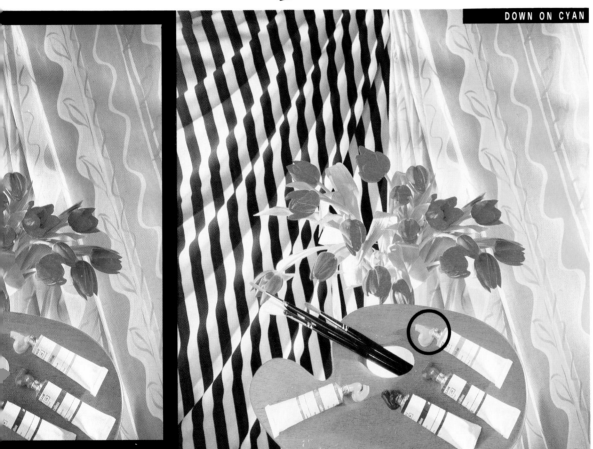

DOWN ON CYAN

If a proof is down on the cyan, the three-colour grey on the colour bar will appear brown. To see if this is caused by the magenta and yellow being up, check the 40% and 80% cyan steps on the colour bar. If they are open, the proof is down on cyan. If these are correct, the fault is in the reproduction.

In this picture, the blues in the curtains look thin and warm, the red flowers have lost all their modelling, and the greys also look warm.

Checking the colour bar You can see that the 40% step has nearly disappeared (left), which shows that the proofing, and not the repro, is at fault.

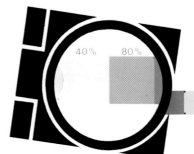

40% 80%

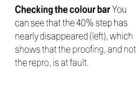

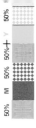

How do I know if the proof is up or down on magenta?

If a proof is up on the magenta, the three-colour grey will have a pink cast. To see if this is caused by the cyan and yellow being down, check the 40% and 80% magenta steps on the colour bar. If they have filled in, the proof is up on magenta. If these are correct, the fault is in the reproduction.

Here, (right) the pinks in the curtain look too strong, the greens look dirty, the yellows are going orange, and all the neutrals in the curtains look pink.

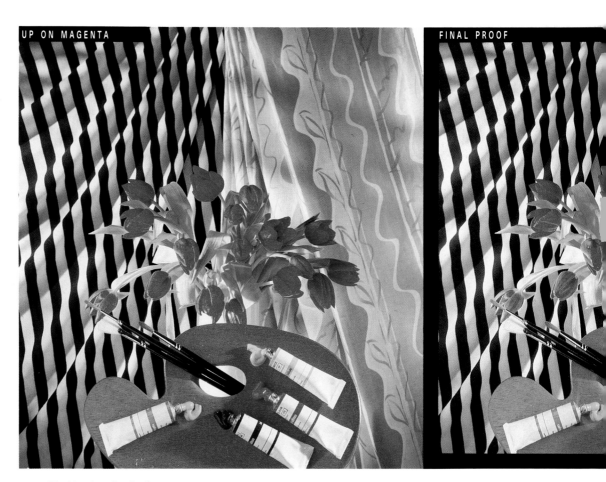

Checking the colour bar You can see that the 40% step is too strong, being nearer 60%, and that the 80% step has filled in solid, showing that the proof has too much magenta ink.

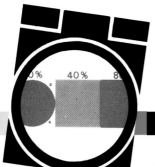

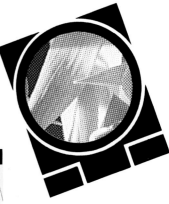

DOWN ON MAGENTA

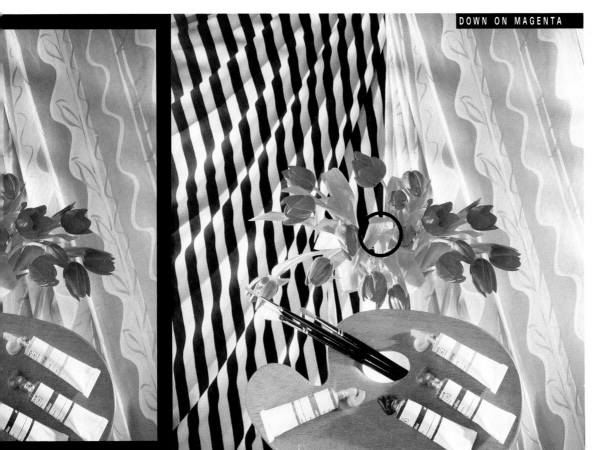

If a proof is down on the magenta, the three-colour grey (below) on the colour bar will appear green. To see if this is caused by the cyan and yellow being up, check the 40% and 80% cyan steps on the colour bar. If they are open, the proof is down on magenta. If these are correct, the fault is in the reproduction.

In this picture (left), the greys in the curtain look green, the greens on the flowers have lost all their modelling, the reds look orange, and the pinks look thin.

Checking the colour bar This shows the green bias on the three-colour neutral step (right). The magenta dot should be only slightly smaller than the cyan dot.

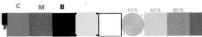

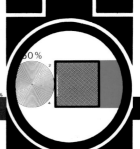
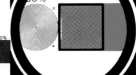

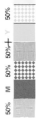

How do I know if the proof is up or down on yellow?

If a proof is up on the yellow, the three-colour grey will have a yellow cast. To see if this is caused by the cyan and magenta being down, check the 40% and 80% yellow steps on the colour bar. If they have filled in, the proof is up on yellow. If these are correct, the fault is in the reproduction.

Here, (right) the neutrals in the picture have a yellow cast, the lighter yellows and greens in the curtains all look too strong, and the reds are slightly orange.

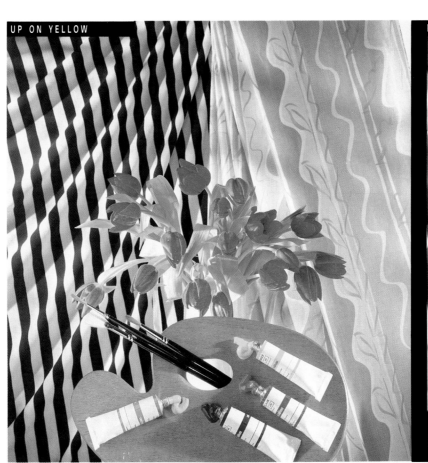

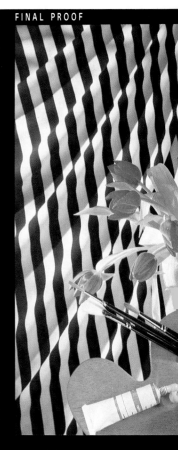

Checking the colour bar
Although the yellow is difficult to see, being such a light colour, this shows the 80% step filling in (right).

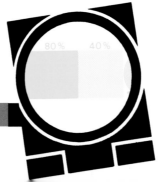

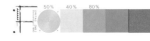

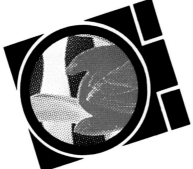

Identifying the problem
Looking at part of the proof through a glass shows the blacks looking mauve, the green leaf has half the yellow required, and there is no yellow dot in the highlight (left).

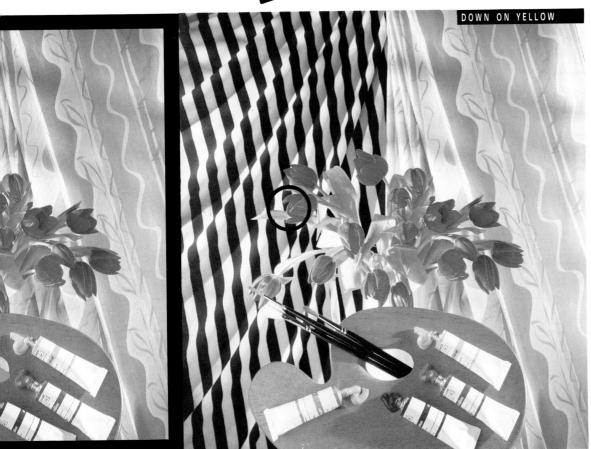

DOWN ON YELLOW

If a proof is down on yellow, the three-colour grey on the colour bar will appear mauve. To see if this is caused by the cyan and magenta being up, check the 40% and 80% yellow steps on the colour bar. If they are open, the proof is down on yellow. If these are correct, the fault is in the reproduction.

In this picture (left), the neutral greys are mauve, the yellows are too weak, the reds look pink, and the greens appear thin and too blue.

Checking the colour bar Here you can see the obvious mauve cast in the three-colour neutral step, showing the lack of yellow ink.

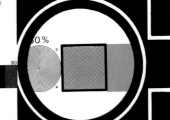

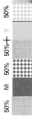

How do I know if the proof is up or down on black?

If a proof is up on the black, check either the 40% and 80% steps on the colour bar to see if they have filled in, or the black on the progressives if they are available. It can be difficult to see this fault on the proof.

Here (right), there is some loss of detail in the shadows, the grey highlights on the side of the paint brushes have started to disappear, and some areas, such as the flowers and neutrals in the curtains, look dirty.

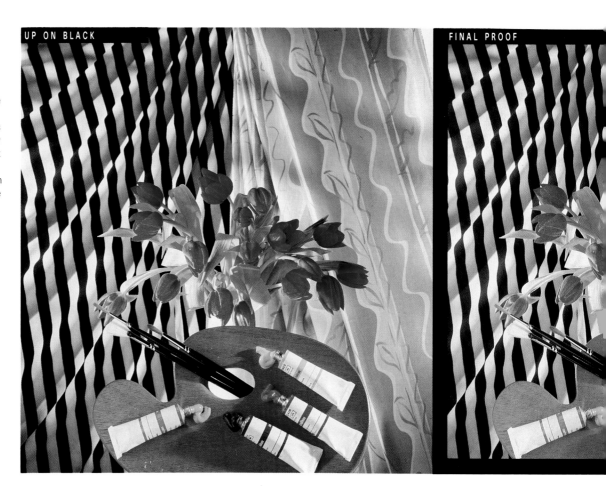

UP ON BLACK

FINAL PROOF

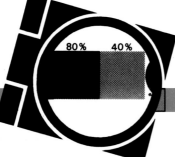

Checking the colour bar
Through a glass you can see that the 80% step has filled in and that the 40% looks too strong. The proof is carrying too much black ink.

80% 40%

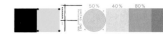

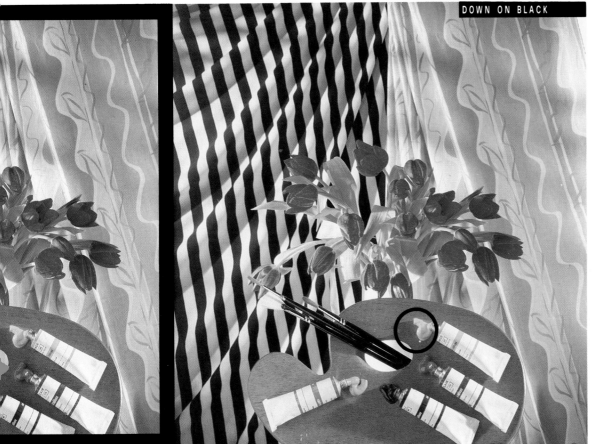

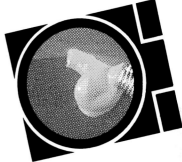

Identifying the problem The black dot on the darker brown is far too small (above). If it was increased to double the size, it would increase the contrast with the lighter brown, which would still not be carrying a black dot.

Here, (left) the shadows in the picture look grey instead of black, and the red flowers and brown of the palette have both lost detail.

If a proof is down on the black, the 40% and 80% steps on the colour bar will look open. Use a linen tester to check this on the colour bar below.

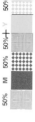

Colour proof correction: fashion and beauty

FIRST PROOF

There are several points that need attention on fashion shots. White fabrics need to be as white as possible, but hold enough to give detail. Black fabrics should be as black as possible, but still be open enough to give detail. It can be difficult to match a fabric – try to supply a swatch of the material to the repro house.

First proof Here, the black dress has filled in, losing detail (**1**); the flesh looks sore (**2**); the white dress looks pink (**3**); and there is also a loss of detail on red dress (**4**).

Instruction to repro Reduce magenta overall; clean up whites; hold detail in black and red dresses.

First proof variations (Above right) Too much yellow makes the highlights look creamy, the blue dress green, and the flesh tones too orange.
(Right) Too much cyan makes the highlights and greys blue. The blue dress is filled in, losing detail in the darker areas. The black dress has a blue cast.
(Below right) Too much black makes the black dress and the bows on the blue dress fill in. The shadows on the knees have filled in. Where there is too much black, it can be difficult to tell, so look at the progressives.
(Bottom right) This generally weak reproduction shows the highlights blown out, losing some of the modelling on the white dress. The black dress looks grey.

Identifying the problem The enlargement shows the predominance of magenta dots. On a neutral highlight area like this, the cyan should be larger than the magenta dots, and the yellow (although difficult to see) should be the same as the magenta.

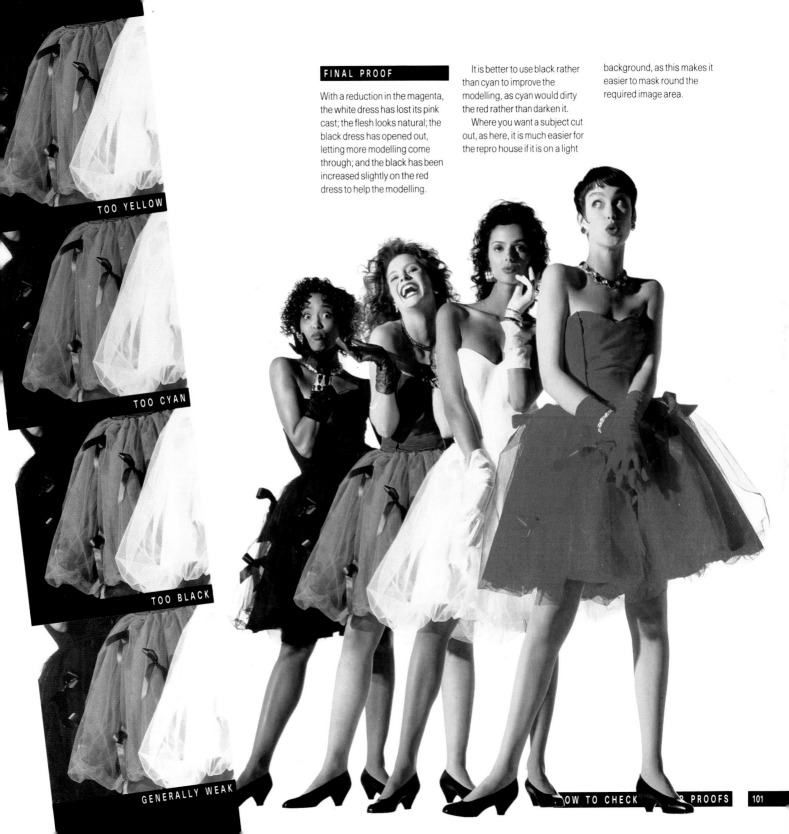

TOO CYAN

TOO BLACK

GENERALLY WEAK

FINAL PROOF

With a reduction in the magenta, the white dress has lost its pink cast; the flesh looks natural; the black dress has opened out, letting more modelling come through; and the black has been increased slightly on the red dress to help the modelling.

It is better to use black rather than cyan to improve the modelling, as cyan would dirty the red rather than darken it.

Where you want a subject cut out, as here, it is much easier for the repro house if it is on a light background, as this makes it easier to mask round the required image area.

Colour proof correction: skin tones

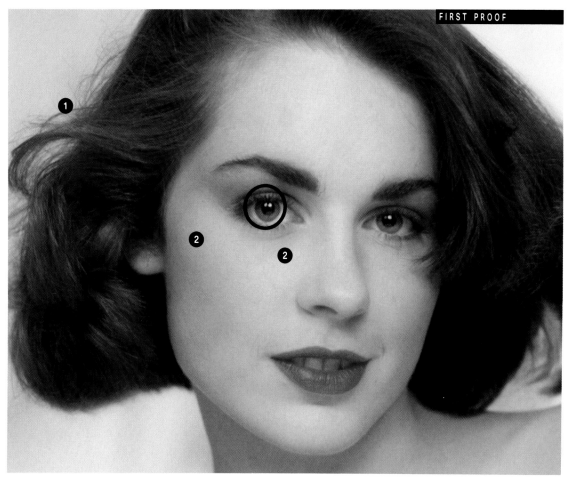

With skin tones, the repro house has to take care to get the right colour balance, as the slightest imbalance can change the picture entirely.

The problem to watch out for with hair is not so much colour (as all hair is different) but fit. As hair consists of thousands of tiny strands, good fit is vital, so the transparency needs to be as sharp as possible.

First proof is flat and un-sharp. The hair has lost detail (**1**); the flesh has lost detail and is soft (**2**).

Instruction to repro Too soft; reduce cyan; improve whites and highlights on eyes.

First proof variations (Top right) The magenta is up, but only in the midtones and shadows. The lighter areas of the flesh are correct, but it becomes sore in the stronger areas. Also, the blue of the eyes is slightly mauve. (Above right) This looks flat. The darker flesh tones are the right colour, but there is no difference between them and the lighter areas which are too full. (Below right) The picture is down in yellow. If you reduced the magenta, the face would lose all its colour, so the yellow has to be increased instead. (Bottom right) This is down in magenta. Reducing the yellow would make the face too pale.

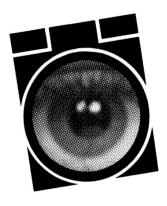

Identifying the problem You can tell the picture is flat by checking the catchlights in the eyes. In a well-reproduced picture, they are paper white, rather than carrying a dot. The same applies to teeth.

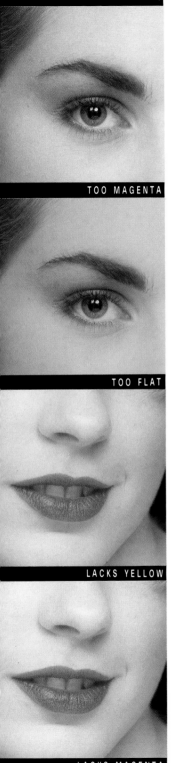

TOO MAGENTA

TOO FLAT

LACKS YELLOW

LACKS MAGENTA

Final proof The importance of the sharpness of the picture is seen below. The detail in the hair has been improved – individual hairs now stand out – as has the skin. The highlights on the lips make them appear glossy.

The white highlights in the eyes have dropped, showing that the tonal range is correct. This has also allowed some of the more subtle colours in the background to come through.

FINAL PROOF

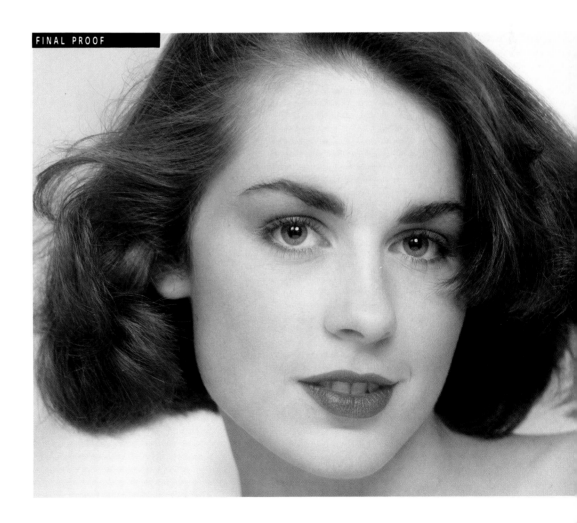

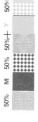

Colour proof correction: skin tones

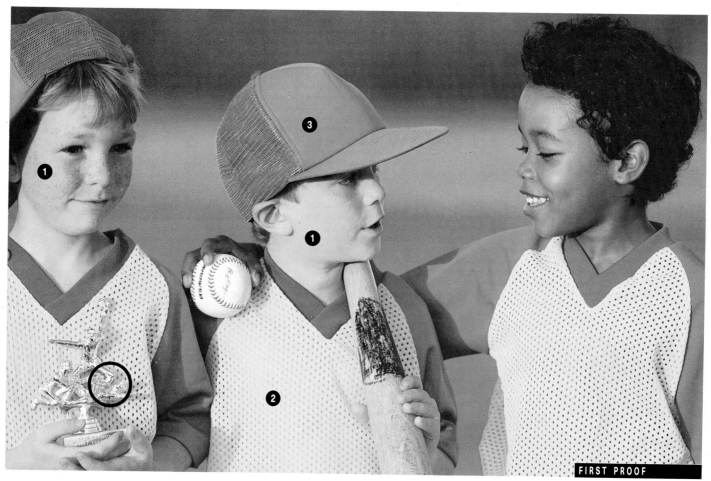

FIRST PROOF

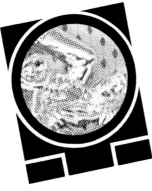

Identifying the problem Using a linen tester to enlarge part of the proof shows the highlights on the chrome are dropping out, but the next tones are also losing highlights in the complementary colours, causing a loss of detail.

First proof This has excessive contrast and generally needs the highlights decreased overall. (It is better to give a general instruction rather than to request decreases in the individual colours – cyan on fleshes; magenta on yellow; magenta and black on greens; and so on.) The exaggerated contrast has over-emphasized the subtle colours of the fleshes (**1**), making the yellows too strong (**2**) and the greens too acid (**3**).

Instruction to repro Reduce contrast overall.

First proof variations (Right) This has too much yellow – the flesh has turned yellow, the slight shadow on the underside of the ball has a yellow cast, and the shirt colour is too strong. (Far right) This is too flat, losing detail in the hat and flesh tones. Also, the ball looks grey instead of white.

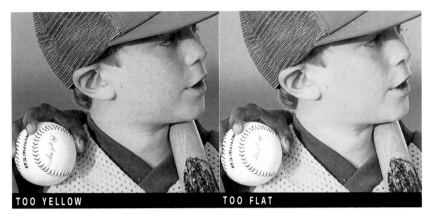

TOO YELLOW TOO FLAT

Final proof With the contrast reduced, the picture becomes less garish. The modelling on the faces and green shirts has been improved, although there has been a slight loss of the exaggerated detail in the highlights, such as the writing on the ball.

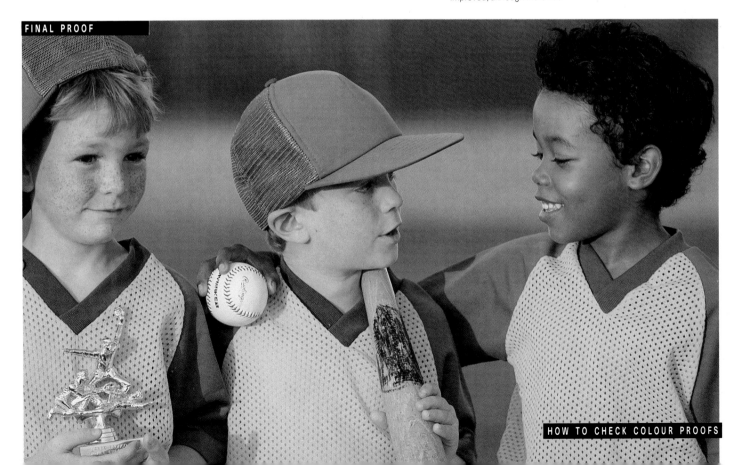

FINAL PROOF

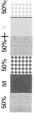

Colour proof correction: food

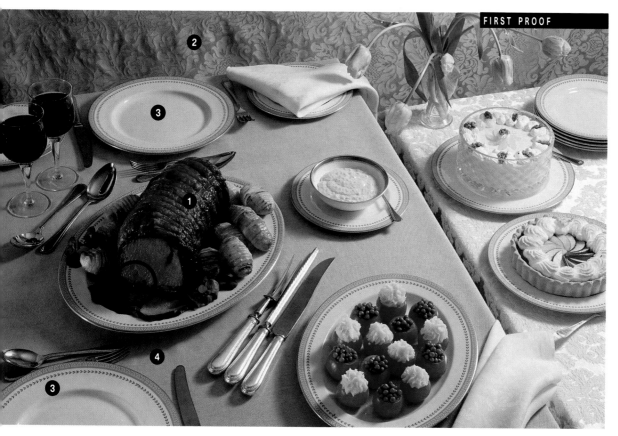

FIRST PROOF

Food is one of the most difficult subjects to reproduce and your instructions to the repro house should be exact. Let them know which is the most important part of the shot. If, as here, it is the sweets, they can then exaggerate the highlight detail, which in turn slightly decreases the midtone detail of the joint.

The food should look appetizing without being too garish. (Meat, for example, can easily look sore and bloody if carrying too much magenta, or pale and insipid if the colours are slightly out of balance.) The most difficult aspect of food reproduction is accurately representing items with subtle or very little colour. Foods that are difficult to reproduce include parsnips, potatoes and dairy produce, whereas peas, carrots and bananas, for example, are much easier as they have strong, identifiable colours. Making sure that the colours do not look false is sometimes more important than matching the transparency exactly.

First proof The cyan is too strong overall causing the top of the roast to look too brown and dirty (**1**); the neutral lace background has a greenish cast (**2**); the neutral greys on the plates are slightly blue (**3**); and the green tablecloth is much too strong (**4**); as the whites and light, creamy colours are correct, it is probably only the midtones which are out of balance.

Instruction to repro Reduce cyan.

Identifying the problem Using a linen tester shows that the blue dots are too large.

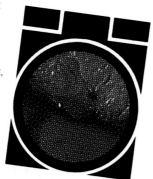

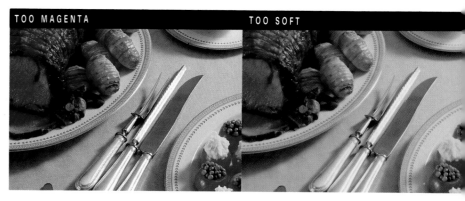

TOO MAGENTA

TOO SOFT

106

Final proof The reduction in cyan has allowed the colour of the joint to come through, and the lace background has lost its greenish tinge.

On the cutlery, you can see a jagged edge caused by the pattern of the dots breaking a straight edge. This unfortunately, is unavoidable. There is also a slight moiré pattern on the tablecloth.

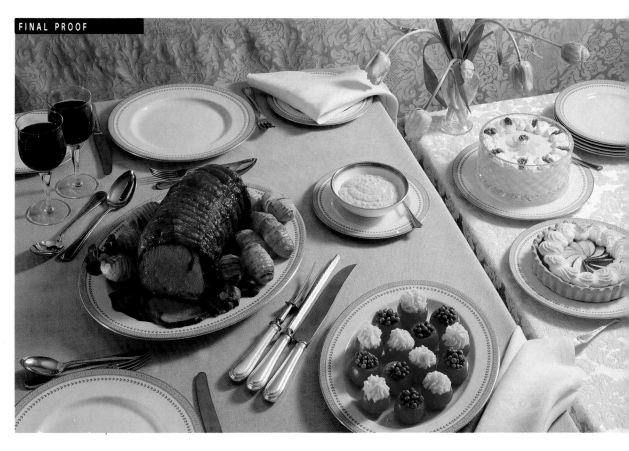

FINAL PROOF

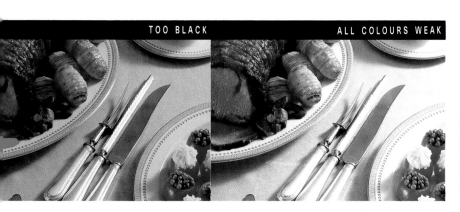

TOO BLACK · ALL COLOURS WEAK

First proof variations (Opposite page, far left) Too much magenta has made the red meat too bloody, and the red on the potatoes looks false. Neutrals have a magenta cast and the green tablecloth looks dirty.

(Opposite page, left) Being too soft has caused a loss of detail overall, especially on the patterned edges of the plates. (This page, far left) Too much black has caused the shadow detail to fill in, most noticeably on the side of the joint.

(This page, left) The highlights are weak and the fine highlight detail is starting to disappear. You can see it on the cutlery, the cream potatoes and the front of the roast. Also, the tablecloth looks pale.

Colour proof correction: food

With dairy produce and ice cream, the difficulty comes in holding detail and definition in what are basically flat white or creamy subjects.

First proof The highlight dots have been set too small. Although the catchlights on the edges of the ice cream should drop out (**1**), the rest should hold a dot for detail (**2**).

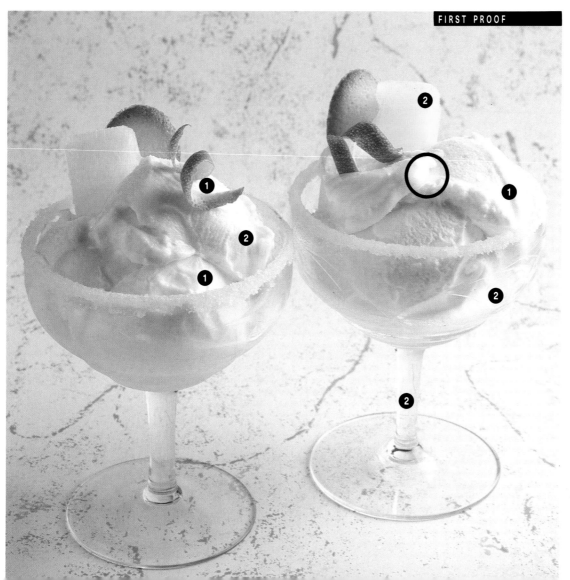

FIRST PROOF

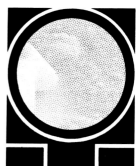

Identifying the problem In the enlarged area (above), only the highlight areas should not be carrying a dot. The enlargement shows that the whole area is too bleached out and does not show enough modelling or detail.

Instruction to repro Increase detail.

Final proof With the highlights increased, the large white areas have disappeared, and both the detail and the texture of the ice cream have been improved. It is difficult to remove all the casts from a white subject, and in this case, the blue in the background gives the ice cream a blue cast.

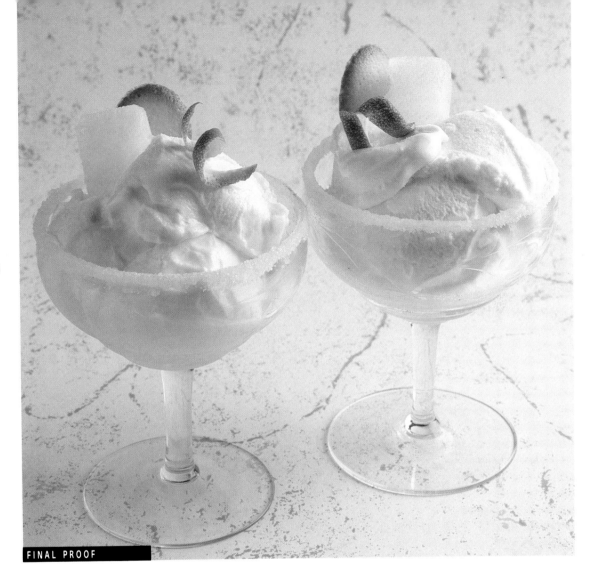

FINAL PROOF

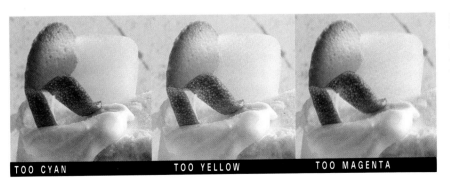

TOO CYAN   TOO YELLOW   TOO MAGENTA

First proof variations (Far left) This has cyan bias, making the greens too strong. The oranges and reds on the biscuit have gone brown, and the yellow looks slightly green.
(Centre left) This is up in yellow, making the reds on the biscuit orange and the ice cream yellow.
(Left) This is too magenta; the ice cream is beginning to turn mauve, the green dirty, and the red edge to the biscuit looks sore.

Colour proof correction: landscapes

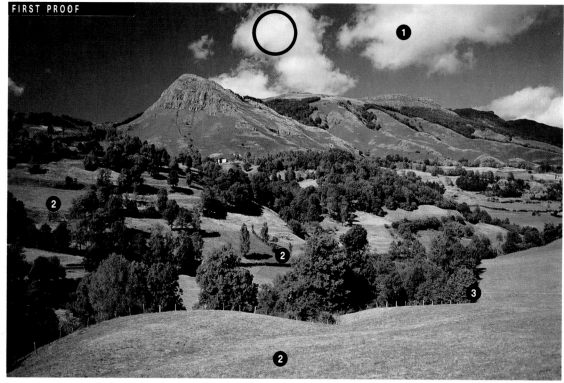

FIRST PROOF

When a sky looks dirty, it is often due to too much yellow. If this is reduced, the sky becomes clearer but slightly lighter. If you increase the cyan and magenta, the sky becomes bluer but darker.

First proof In this case, the picture is too flat overall, making the clouds look dirty and grey (**1**). If the highlight dots are made smaller, it will also help the definition between the beiges (**2**) and greens (**3**). This is done by reducing the cyan highlights in the beige and the magenta highlights in the green.

Instruction to repro Brighten highlights.

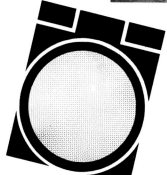

Identifying the problem The enlargement shows the highlight in the clouds. The magenta and yellow dots should be as small as possible, with the cyan dots only slightly bigger. Here, they are all too big.

First proof variations (Below left) With the yellow slightly down, the grey rocks look mauve and the clouds have mauve edges. Reducing the cyan and magenta would only make the picture look thin.
(Below right) The lack of

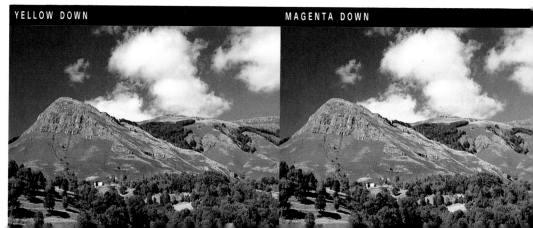

YELLOW DOWN

MAGENTA DOWN

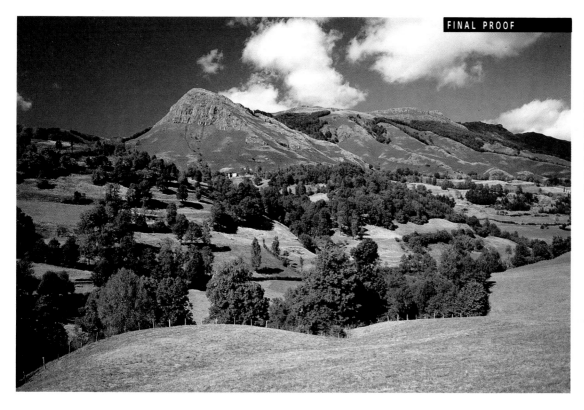

Final proof Here, the colour balance is the same as the first proof, but the range of the picture has been increased by making the highlight dots smaller. This has made the picture look much sharper, with greater detail and definition.

magenta has given the sky a green cast. In fact, all the greens are too strong.
(Below left) The greens are all too heavy and the sky is too dark, so ask for the cyan and the yellow to be reduced.
(Below right) Although the colour balance is correct, there is not enough difference between the dark greens and the shadows, so the black should be increased.

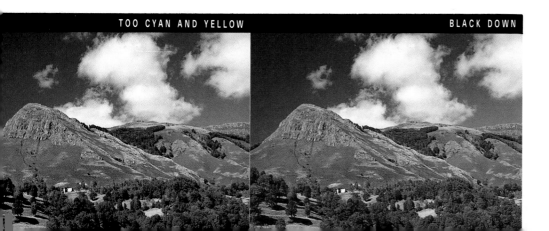

TOO CYAN AND YELLOW BLACK DOWN

Colour proof correction: landscapes

Grass and foliage can be difficult subjects to reproduce correctly. The predominant colours are obviously cyan and yellow, but the balance between them needs to be just right – there is a danger that the subject can become too blue or yellow.

Magenta is also important as it helps to give detail, but too much of it will make the grass or foliage dirty and brown. If you want the grass to be darker, but not to become dirty, then increase the black. Increasing the black will also help foliage with dark reds, mauves, browns and blues in their colouring. It makes it darker without affecting the general colour.

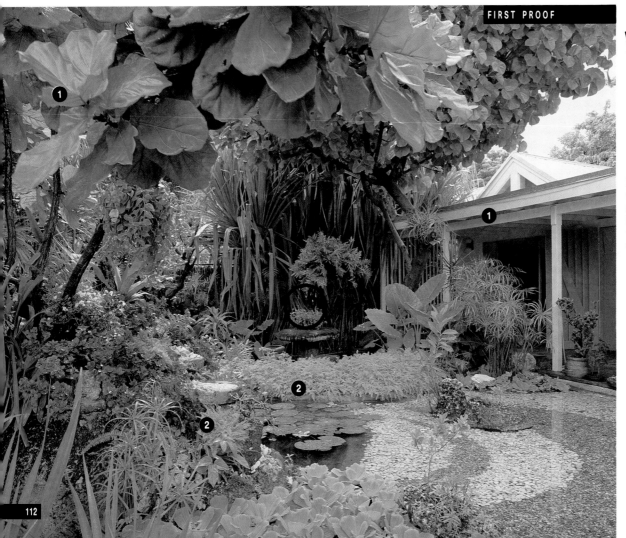

FIRST PROOF

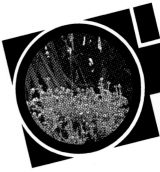

Identifying the problem The enlargement shows the large cyan dots on the pink flowers are killing the magenta, so making them dull. Reducing cyan will let the magenta come through.

First proof The cyan is too strong, giving everything a cyan cast (**1**) and killing all the fine detail in the greens (**2**). Increasing the other colours will only lose more detail.

Instruction to repro Reduce cyan.

Final proof The only difference to the first proof here is a reduction of cyan. As a result, detail has been improved and the modelling on the foliage is clearer, allowing more colours to come through.

The stones in the pool now look a warm brown and the whites on the building are neutral. The best way of telling if any of the colours are out of balance is to look at the neutral grey, such as the rocks in this picture.

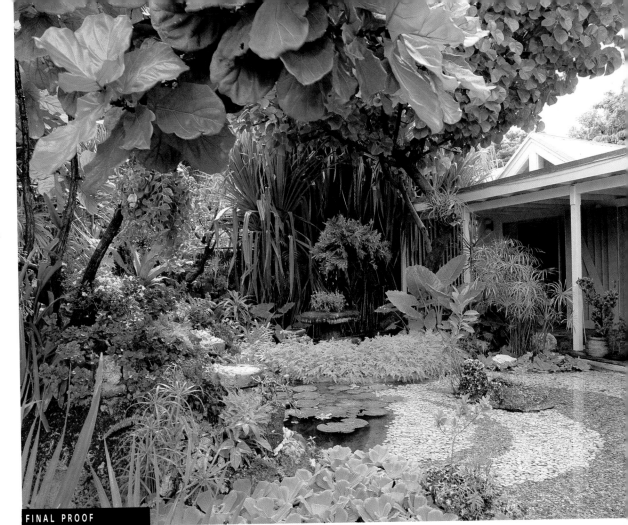

FINAL PROOF

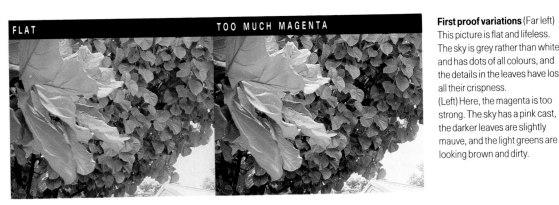

FLAT   TOO MUCH MAGENTA

First proof variations (Far left) This picture is flat and lifeless. The sky is grey rather than white and has dots of all colours, and the details in the leaves have lost all their crispness.
(Left) Here, the magenta is too strong. The sky has a pink cast, the darker leaves are slightly mauve, and the light greens are looking brown and dirty.

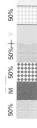

Colour proof correction: landscapes

In general, clients are not too worried about matching travel shots with the original so long as the printed result is a bright, appealing picture. It is important to tell the repro house if you want to improve on the original,

otherwise they will attempt to match it.

First proof Even if this proof matches the original, it is not suitable for a holiday brochure – the beach looks dirty (**1**); the

clouds look dull (**2**); the sky is not blue (**3**); and the greens are too dark and lack detail (**4**).

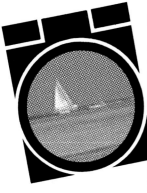

Identifying the problem This enlargement shows dots in the white sail. These should be dropped out to make the sail whiter, and therefore stand out from the background.

Instruction to repro Brighten overall.

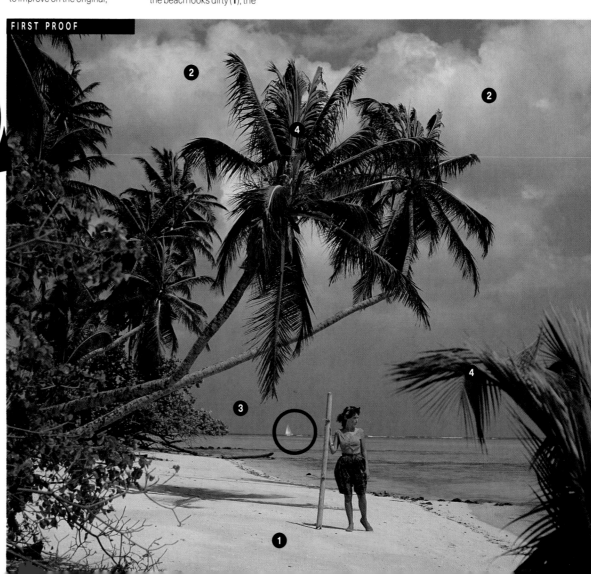

FIRST PROOF

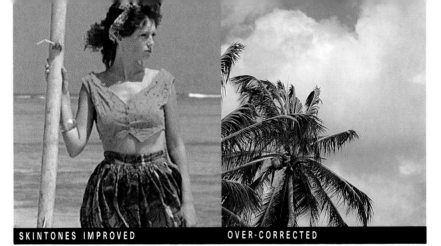

First proof variation (Right) This shows the improvement on the skintones, which looked sore and sunburnt on the first proof. The girl's top might be the wrong colour, but it is not a critical error.

SKINTONES IMPROVED   OVER-CORRECTED

First proof variation (Left) This has been over-corrected. The clouds now look thin and the sky looks grey, or even slightly green, instead of blue.

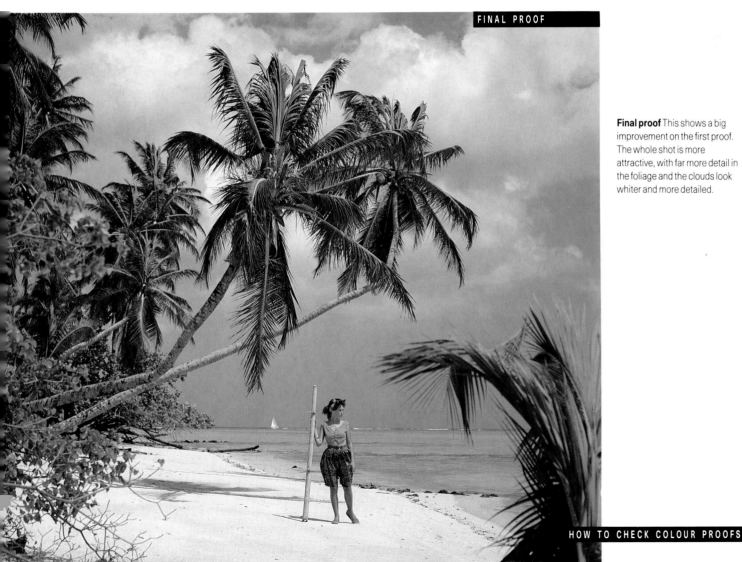

FINAL PROOF

Final proof This shows a big improvement on the first proof. The whole shot is more attractive, with far more detail in the foliage and the clouds look whiter and more detailed.

Colour proof correction: landscapes

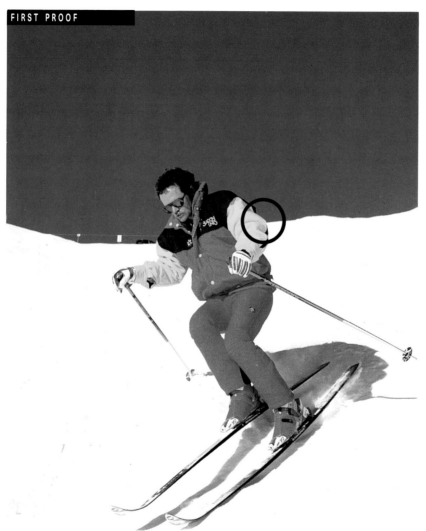

FIRST PROOF

First proof On skiing shots, the snow can present quite a problem. Snow is not paper white as it always has a reflected colour and, when reproduced, it can be difficult to make the snow white enough, while keeping a big enough dot to keep the snow's detail. In this case, the highlight dots have been set too small, causing the snow to look blown out.

Instruction to repro snow looks blown out; increase detail .

Identifying the problem In the enlargement below you can see that there are no dots at all in the snow.

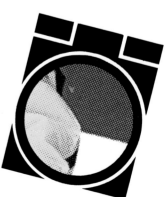

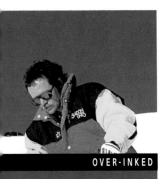

OVER-INKED

First proof variations (Left) Here the shadows are too strong, causing a loss of detail in all the dark areas.

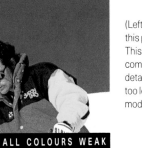

ALL COLOURS WEAK

(Left) Detail has also been lost on this proof, but in the highlights. This has made the complementary colours that give detail on the red and yellow to be too low, thus losing the modelling.

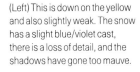

LACKS YELLOW

(Left) This is down on the yellow and also slightly weak. The snow has a slight blue/violet cast, there is a loss of detail, and the shadows have gone too mauve.

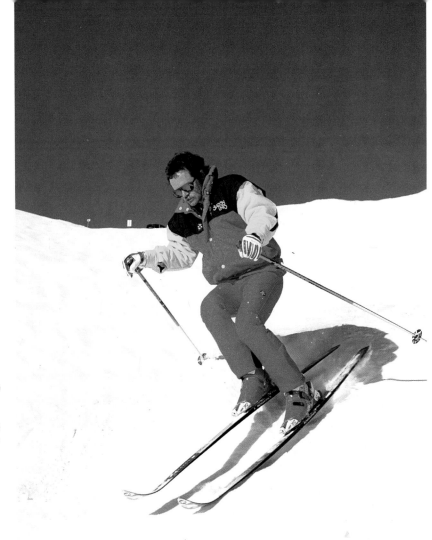

FINAL PROOF

Final proof With stronger highlights, the modelling on the snow has been improved, as it has on the clothing.

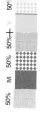

Colour proof correction: cars

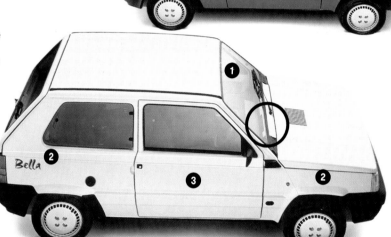

The special colours (which are sometimes metallic) used on the paintwork of cars can be difficult to match using four colours.

To get the maximum detail on the moulding of the car body and lights, the scanner operator needs to set the scanner on the car, which sometimes means sacrificing the background.

It is vital that the transparencies for car photographs are pin sharp. If an image is not sharp enough, reproduction cannot hold the detail; the repro house can do nothing to improve it.

First proof This looks soft (**1**), losing the modelling on the white car especially (**2**). The cars have a yellow bias, which makes them look dull (**3**).

Instruction to repro Reduce yellow; improve fit; retouch shadows to give soft edges.

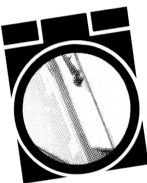

Identifying the problem In the magnified image above you can see the importance of fit. The magenta is out of fit, making the picture look soft and un-sharp.

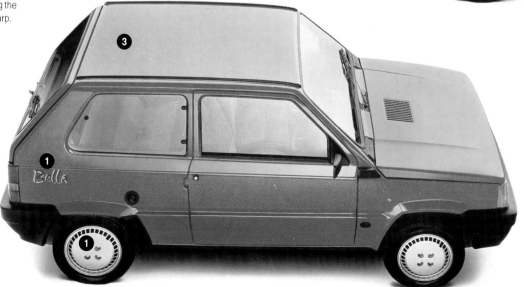

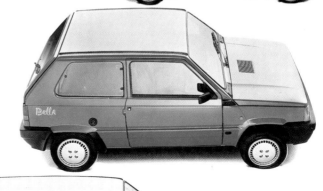

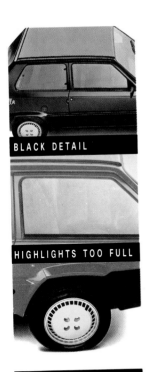

BLACK DETAIL

HIGHLIGHTS TOO FULL

TOO YELLOW

Final proof With a reduction of the yellow, and the general sharpening of the image, the modelling and definition in the bodywork have been improved. The shadows under the cars have been retouched to give soft edges. When shadows are cut out on white, they look better if reproduced only in black. There is some moiré patterning on the bonnet grilles which is unavoidable.

First proof variations (Top) Here, the shadows are too full. (Middle) In this case, the highlights are too full, causing a loss of detail in the interior of the car. (Bottom) This picture is too yellow. The reds have gone slightly orange and the chromes look warm.

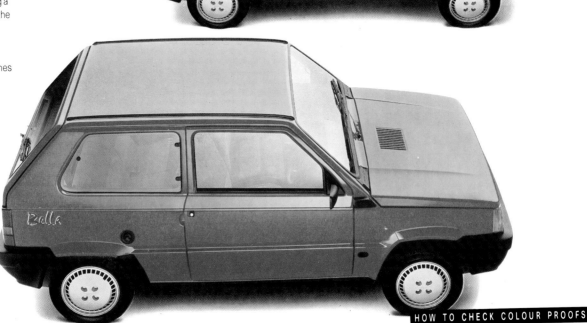

Colour proof correction: cars

First proof This picture has been taken under a yellow awning causing all the reflections on the car to appear too yellow (**1**). The designer should have asked the repro house to reduce this, but without this request, they assumed that they should follow the transparency. It now has to be altered at proof stage, and would therefore be an "author's correction", chargeable to the client.

When reproducing chrome, the best results are achieved by dropping the highlights out to paper white. This has been done here, but has affected the rest of the picture by causing the whites above the car to lose some of their detail.

Instruction to repro Reduce yellow.

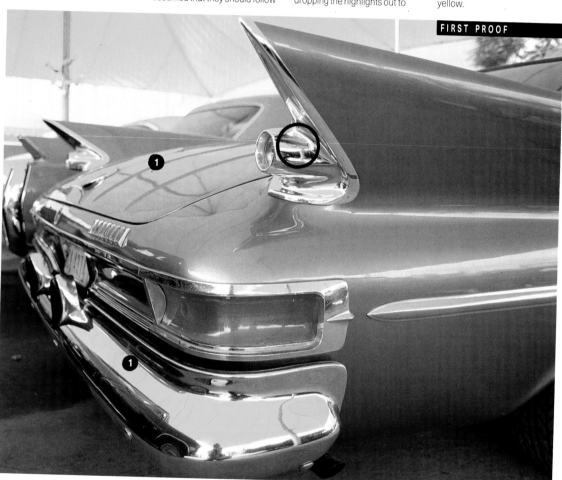

FIRST PROOF

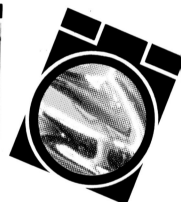

Identifying the problem
Looking at an area of the proof through a linen tester shows the highlights on the chrome have dropped out to white. If there were any dots in the chrome, it would look dull and flat.

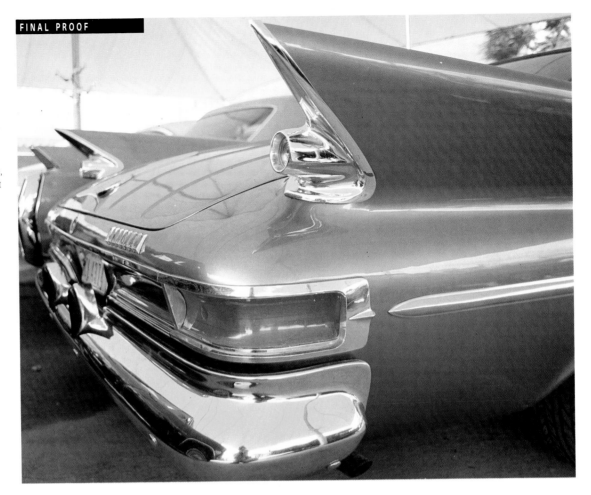

Final proof Having reduced the overall predominance of yellow, the car looks more natural. Here, the browns and beiges have lost some yellow and look more natural. This also allows more detail and modellling to come through.

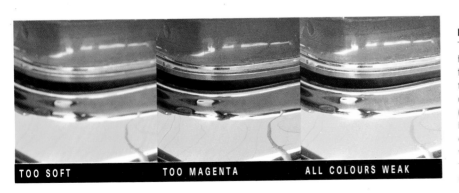

TOO SOFT   TOO MAGENTA   ALL COLOURS WEAK

First proof variations (Far left) The softness has made the highlights on the red light look fuzzy and un-sharp. The red tones on the yellow have virtually disappeared.
(Centre left) Too much magenta has made the yellows take on an orange hue. The brown looks too warm and the shadow detail in the red light is disappearing.
(Left) Although the colour balance in the brown is correct here, the overall weakness of colour makes the picture look too light. This has also meant that the fine lines in the yellow are disappearing.

Colour proof correction: interiors

Furniture can be difficult to reproduce, as a slight imbalance of any colour can change the shade of the wood entirely.
First proof This picture is badly lit, with the top being too light (**1**) while the bottom is in shadow (**2**). The highlight dot needs to be set slightly bigger, but not so much as to lose detail. The proof is also down on the magenta making the wood too yellow (**3**) and garish .

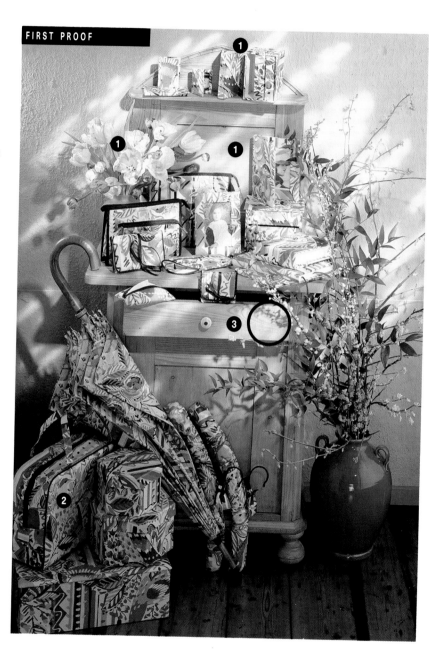

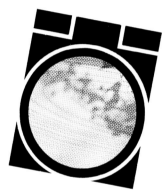

Identifying the problem The lines on the wood are short of magenta, causing the wood to lose its texture and detail (above). The cyan dot in the darker areas is too small because the picture has too much contrast.

Instruction to repro Reduce highlights; increase magenta.

Final proof With slightly larger dots in the highlights, the detail in the top half and lighter areas of the picture has been improved, and the modelling of the wood is much better. Reducing the cyan and yellow shadow while increasing the magenta slightly has made the bottom half of the picture less dense and slightly warmer.

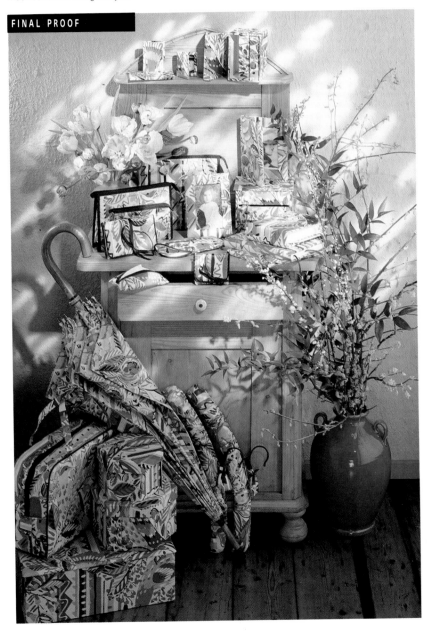

FINAL PROOF

TOO MUCH CONTRAST

SHADOWS FILLED IN

First proof variations (Top) This has too much contrast – the highlights have dropped out, losing all detail.
(Above) The magenta has been increased, but the cyan and yellow shadows are too heavy, which has filled in the darker areas.

Colour proof correction: interiors

The main problem with a white subject is that it often looks flat and uninteresting. Very little detail or modelling comes across. Any slight imbalance of colour can cause a cast, and shadows falling across the subject will have a colour cast. Using an increased black can give more shape and modelling. Take care with backlit subjects such as this one, as they have false highlights.

First proof The black here is too strong, causing everything to look black (**1**) and dirty (**2**).

Instruction to repro Reduce black; lighten highlights.

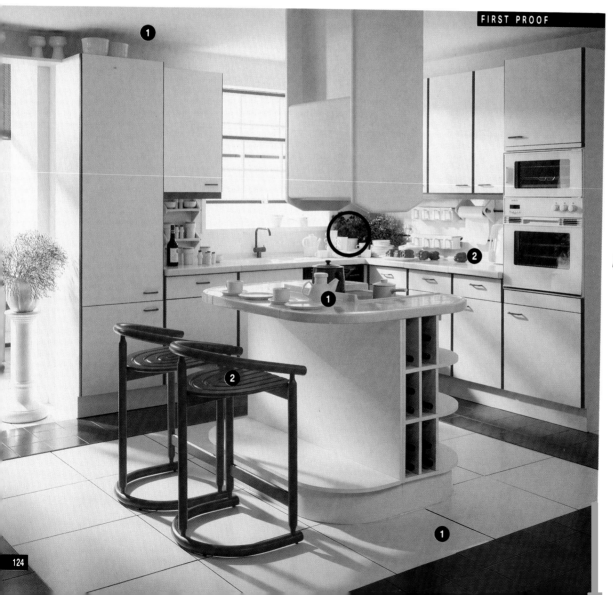

FIRST PROOF

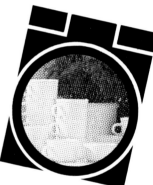

Identifying the problem Using a linen tester to examine the proof shows the black dots on the red making the picture look dull.

Final proof This shows a reduction in the black. Also the repro house have lightened the highlights by making a slight reduction in the highlight dot of the other colours to compensate for the backlighting.

The reduction in the black has allowed the richness in the red floor tiles and the stools to come through. You can now see that the handles on the units are red, which were previously obscured by too much black.

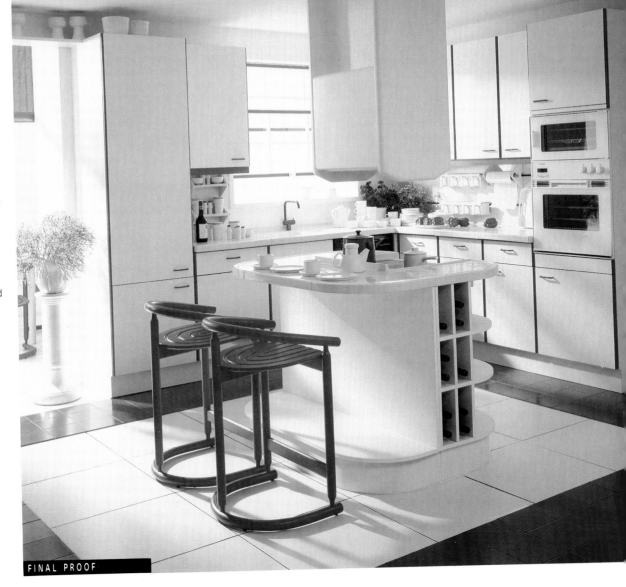

FINAL PROOF

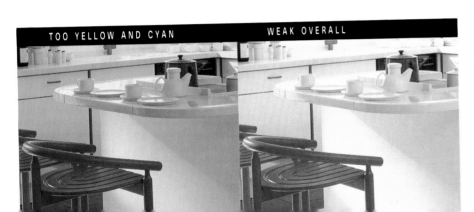

TOO YELLOW AND CYAN

WEAK OVERALL

First proof variations (Far left) This reproduction has a bias of cyan and yellow, making the neutrals green. The red chair now looks brown.
(Left) This is too light overall and the reflections on the table top have been lost completely.

Colour proof correction: jewellery

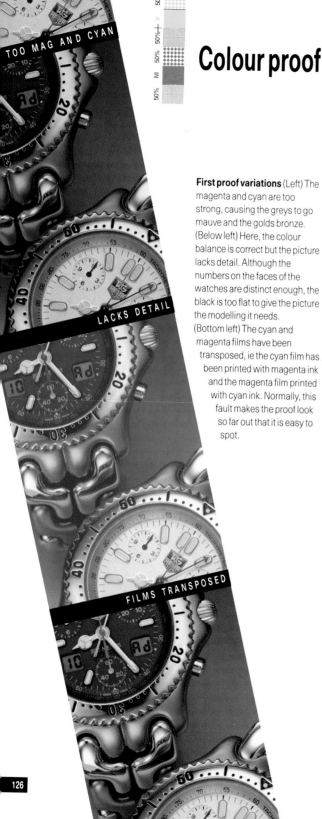

TOO MAG AND CYAN

LACKS DETAIL

FILMS TRANSPOSED

First proof variations (Left) The magenta and cyan are too strong, causing the greys to go mauve and the golds bronze. (Below left) Here, the colour balance is correct but the picture lacks detail. Although the numbers on the faces of the watches are distinct enough, the black is too flat to give the picture the modelling it needs. (Bottom left) The cyan and magenta films have been transposed, ie the cyan film has been printed with magenta ink and the magenta film printed with cyan ink. Normally, this fault makes the proof look so far out that it is easy to spot.

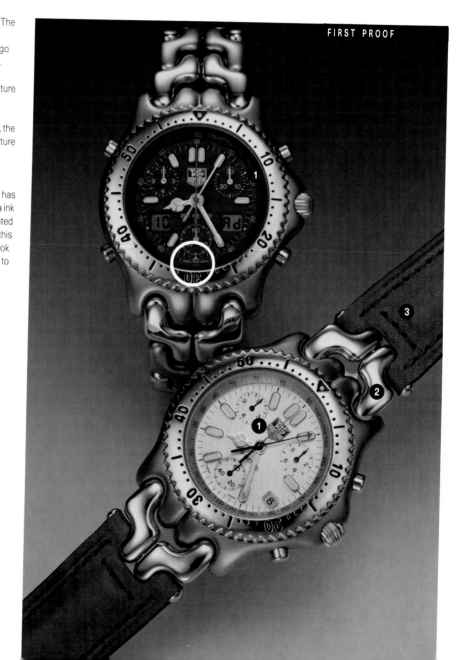

FIRST PROOF

With jewellery shots, it is important that the original is as sharp as possible to keep the definition when reproduced.

First proof This proof does not look very sharp (**1**); the golds look dull (**2**); as does the leather strap (**3**).

Instruction to repro Increase contrast; reduce cyan; strengthen yellow.

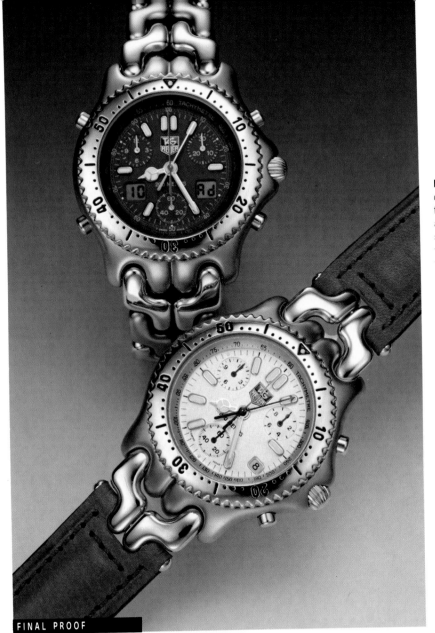

FINAL PROOF

Final proof Increasing the contrast has corrected all three faults in the first proof: the golds are a lot brighter; the leather strap is much cleaner; and the whole picture is sharper. There is far more detail and everything is legible.

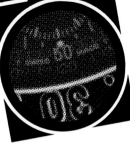

Identifying the problem
Looking at the problem proof through a glass shows that it is too flat – the white line should only have a yellow dot in it.

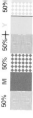

Colour proof correction: fine art

FIRST PROOF

Reproducing fine art is difficult for a repro house as it will normally only see a transparency, not the original. The transparency should always be shot and reproduced with step wedges, as here.

First proof By looking at the step wedge, you can see at a glance that the cyan on this proof is down. This has made all the blues (**1**), greens (**2**) and browns (**3**) look thin.

Instruction to repro Increase cyan.

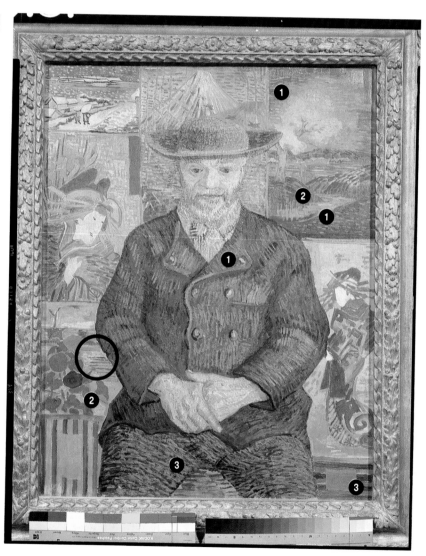

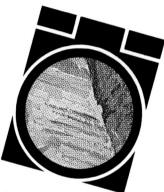

Identifying the problem In the enlargement (above) you can see the lack of cyan in the greens. With this shade of green, the dots should nearly join up.

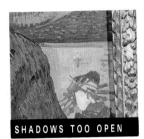

SHADOWS TOO OPEN

First proof variation (Above)
The shadows are too open, and the darker blues too light, causing a loss of detail and modelling.

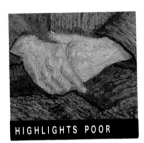

HIGHLIGHTS POOR

First proof variation (Above)
This picture is also flat, but in this case the highlight dots are too large, causing a loss of detail in the lighter areas and over-emphasizing the slightly darker highlights. The effect has been to make the hands slightly green.

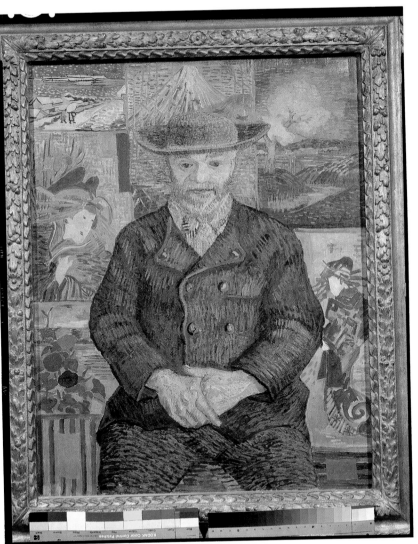

You could use the step wedge alone to check the correction achieved on this proof. The greys are now neutral; the greens are stronger and less yellow; and the browns are less warm.

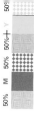

Colour proof correction: illustration

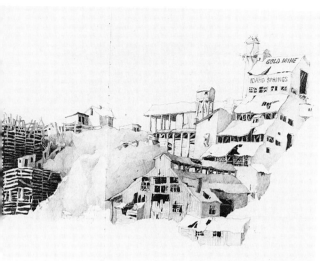

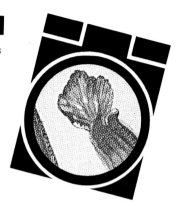

Pictures containing text, such as this (below), can tend to look flat and illegible as it is made up of dots of all four colours.
Identifying the problem In the enlargement (right), you can see the problem. The fine lines in the picture are less than a dot in width, and thus lose definition.

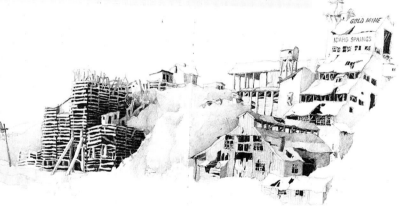

FIRST PROOF

(Top) This black and white halftone is too flat, which makes the background look grey instead of white. The flatness also accounts for the loss of detail.

FINAL PROOF

(Above) Here, the dot in the background has been made smaller, thus increasing the contrast between the highlights and the midtones (ie 50%). This gives the image greater detail.

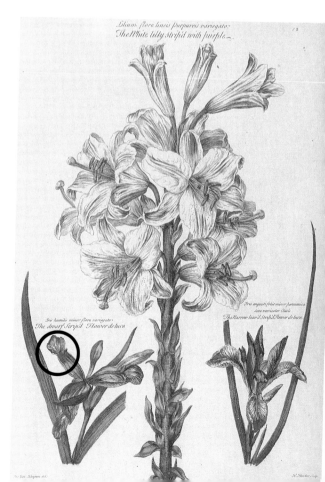

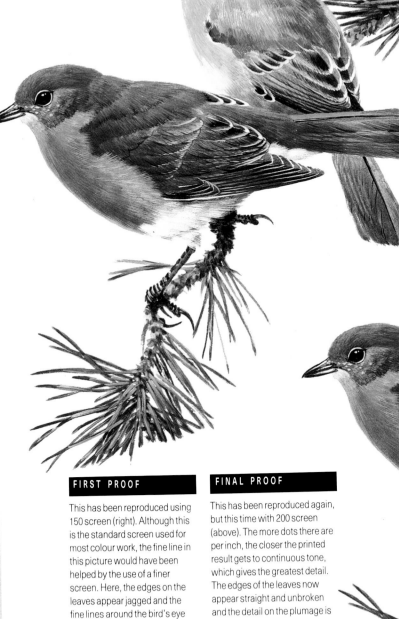

FINAL PROOF

The text has become far more legible and the definition of the plants improved by using a black line instead of tone (below). Obviously, this should be an instruction to the repro house at the outset or you will be charged for an "author's correction".

When enlarged, you can see how the improvement has been achieved by the line shot giving enhanced detail.

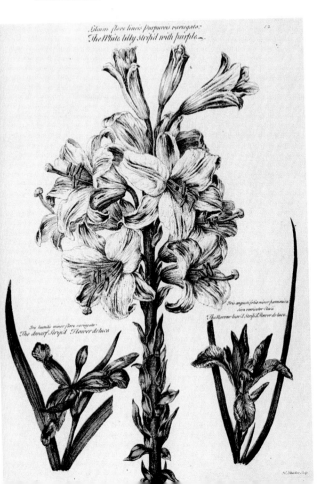

FIRST PROOF

This has been reproduced using 150 screen (right). Although this is the standard screen used for most colour work, the fine line in this picture would have been helped by the use of a finer screen. Here, the edges on the leaves appear jagged and the fine lines around the bird's eye are not picking up sufficiently.

FINAL PROOF

This has been reproduced again, but this time with 200 screen (above). The more dots there are per inch, the closer the printed result gets to continuous tone, which gives the greatest detail. The edges of the leaves now appear straight and unbroken and the detail on the plumage is greatly enhanced.

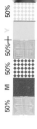

What are the problems in reversing out and overprinting type?

TYPE SHOULD BE reversed out of as few colours as possible. Any type matter smaller than 10pt should be reversed out of one colour only. This is because exact positioning cannot be guaranteed in printing.

If it is necessary to reverse out of two or more colours, it may be advisable to use the dominant colour (black, for example) for the shape of the letters. However, this method can only be used when there is a solid black. If it is done with colour tints, the spreading will give a halo on the colours that are not spread.

Also, whenever you use a solid black, there should be a 50% tint of cyan under it, to give a depth of colour. Although it is helpful to specify this, usually the repro house will do it anyway.

Very small letters and typefaces which are light or have serifs should not be used for reversals, as the slightest misregister (printing out of position) will result in fringes showing colour in the white type areas.

The designer should also ensure that reversed-out lettering on light backgrounds is legible.

FOREIGN CO-EDITIONS In book production there are often co-editions with foreign publishers and these can only be economical if the black plate alone is changed. Obviously if type is reversed out of one or more of the other colours this would involve changing extra plates which could make the co-edition uneconomical.

OVERPRINTING Care should be taken by the designer when overprinting type matter that it should not merge into a light or dark background, as this will affect legibility.

Trying out type The strip of type (below) running across this spread demonstrates what works and does not work when type is reversed out of, and overprints, certain colours.

m nonnumy eiusmod tempor incidunt lore magna aliqua erat volupat. Ut en: eniam, quis nostrud exercitation nisi ra commodo consequat. Duis autem v lor in reprehenderit in volupante velit es nsequat, vel illum dolore eu fugiat nu ero eos et accusam et iusto odiom digr

Lrem ipsum dolor sit amet, consectetur adipiscir elit, sed diam zum nonnumy eiusmod temp incidunt ut labore et dolore magna aliqua er volupat. Ut enim ad minim veniam, quis nostru exercitation nisi ut aliquip ex era commodo cons quat. Duis autem vel eum irure dolor in reprehende in volupante velit esse molestaie consequat, vel illu dolore eu fugiat nulla pariatur. At vero eos accusam et iusto odiom dignissim qui bland praesent luptatum delenit aigue duos dolor et molestias excepteur sint occaecat cupidtat no provident, simil sunt it culpa qui officia deseru mollit anim id est laborum et dolor fuga. Et harum

New York
New York
New York
New York
New York
New York
New York
New York
New York
New York
New York
New York
New York
New York

When is type poor?

WHEN CHECKING the quality of type on colour proofs, the designer should look out for:

Type that is too weak and grey or breaking up – caused by overexposure. Type that is too strong and thickened – caused by underexposure. Paste-up marks show – caused by the paste-up not having been cleaned properly or the repro house not "spotting" the negative to remove marks.

FINE LETTERING Thin lines, box rules and medium and fine type matter and detail should ideally be reproduced in only one colour. The use of two or more colours will make it difficult for the printer to ensure that they are exactly on top of each other and any movement during printing (which cannot always be avoided on high-speed presses) will result in the subject being out of register, so that fringes are seen.

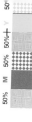

How do I deal with originals and proofs for packaging?

IN THIS BOOK we have dealt mainly with the litho process and with printing on paper or board. Packaging can involve other printing processes such as gravure, screen printing or flexography, all of which are described in the introduction. It can also involve printing on glass, flexible or solid plastic, wood, metal and other materials.

As a result of the wide range of processes and materials, there are many different ways in which artwork should be prepared and proofs checked. Because this is a specialist area, the designer needs to work much more closely with the repro house and printer than is necessary with litho jobs.

For example, cartons which contain milk or orange juice are made out of a waterproofed board which cannot be printed by lithography and is therefore printed by flexography (see pages 28-29). In flexography, a photopolymer plate is used and the process is such that it is difficult or impossible to show fine type. If the artwork has fine type on it, this will thicken up so as to be unrecognizable, and the same will happen to fine rules and other graphic details. Reversed-out small or fine type will tend to fill in.

PRINTING PROCESSES

Glass
Onto paper labels
- Lithographic
- Gravure
- Letterpress
- Silkscreen

Onto PVC shrink sleeves
- Gravure reverse printed
- Flexographic reverse printed

Plastic
Onto paper labels
- Processes as for glass
Shrink sleeves
- As above
Stretch labels
- As above
In mould labelling
- i.e. special type of pre-printed label inserted into bottle mould
  Bottle is formed so label is fused to bottle surface

Therimage
- Heat transfer labels
  Gravure and screenprint
  Dry-offset.

Cardboard
- Lithographic
- Flexographic
- Screenprint
- Gravure

Plastic
Direct onto plastic
- Screenprint
- Flexographic

Foil/film Laminates
- Flexographic
- Gravure

Can/metal
- Dry-offset print
- Reprotherm – transfer system for full-colour photographic image

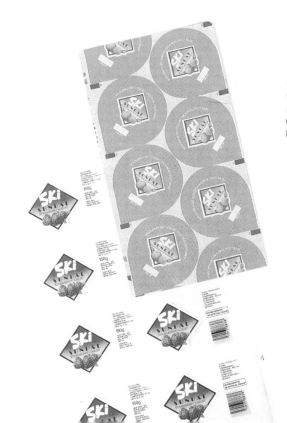

Printed sheets for yoghurt cartons. The containers are printed on specially treated (waterproofed) board and the lids on metallic foil (left).

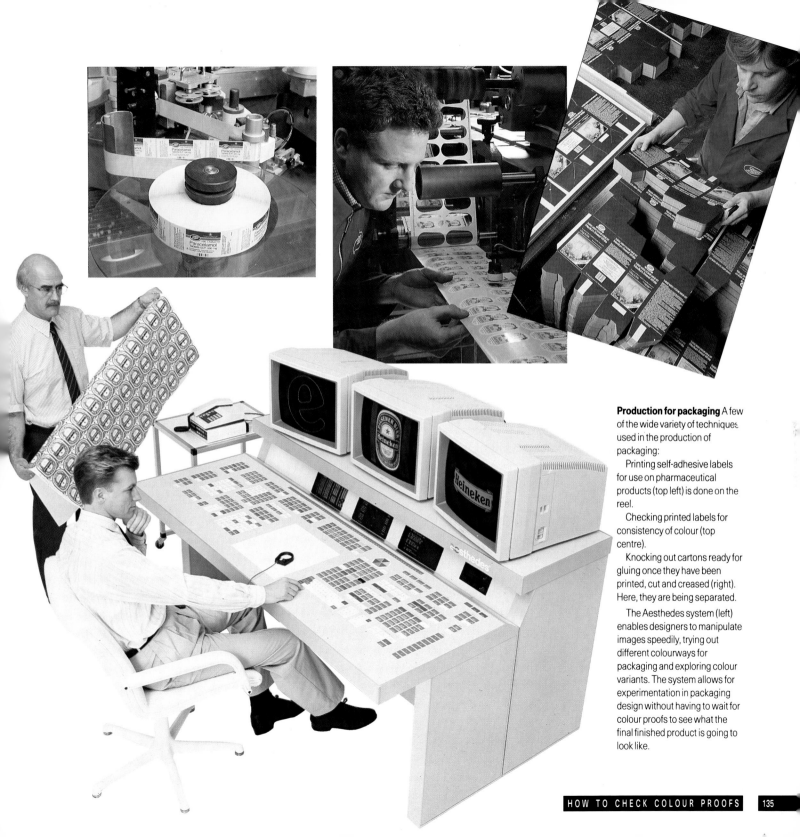

Production for packaging A few of the wide variety of techniques used in the production of packaging:

Printing self-adhesive labels for use on pharmaceutical products (top left) is done on the reel.

Checking printed labels for consistency of colour (top centre).

Knocking out cartons ready for gluing once they have been printed, cut and creased (right). Here, they are being separated.

The Aesthedes system (left) enables designers to manipulate images speedily, trying out different colourways for packaging and exploring colour variants. The system allows for experimentation in packaging design without having to wait for colour proofs to see what the final finished product is going to look like.

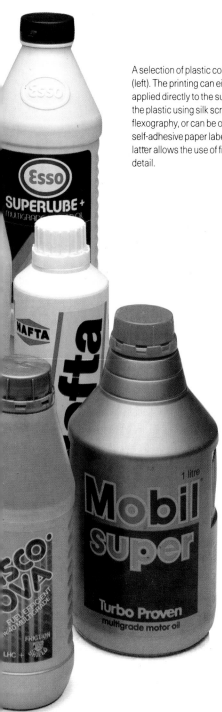

A selection of plastic containers (left). The printing can either be applied directly to the surface of the plastic using silk screen or flexography, or can be offset on a self-adhesive paper label. The latter allows the use of finer detail.

A typical pack for liquids (right). This is an Elopak container made of board sandwiched between layers of polyethylene (below). Liquid packs can also be lined with foil for fruit juice packaging.

Printing on this material is either by flexography or gravure. Both these processes have limitations as regards register and the use of fine type. The designer needs to work closely with the printer to achieve good results.

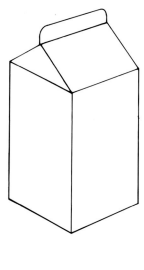

Here, the black rules round the type overlap the colour area to minimize register problems and avoid white showing round the lettering.

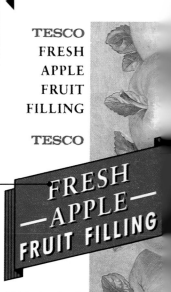

TESCO
FRESH
APPLE
FRUIT
FILLING

TESCO

FRESH APPLE FRUIT FILLING

Lightly stewed apple, delicious with cream or custard. Ideal as a pie filling. All the taste of fresh apples in a convenient pack.

500 g ℮

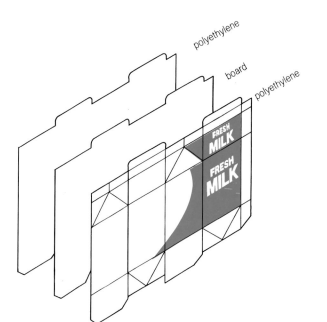

polyethylene

board

polyethylene

FRESH MILK

FRESH MILK

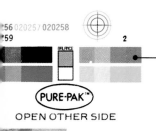

INGREDIENTS:
Apple, Water, Sugar, Modified Starch, Glucose Syrup.

TESCO QUALITY
If you are not entirely satisfied with any Tesco product, please return it to the store where it was purchased where we will be pleased to replace it. Or send it with the packaging to the Consumer Relations Manager at the following address, stating where and when it was purchased. This offer does not affect your statutory rights.
PRODUCED IN THE U.K. FOR TESCO STORES LTD., CHESHUNT, EN8 9SL © TESCO '89 0477

NUTRITION		
A serving = approx. ¼ of the carton		
TYPICAL COMPOSITION	A 125g (4½ oz) serving provides	100g (3½ oz) provide
Energy	314 kJ/ 75 kcal	251 kJ/ 60 kcal
Protein	0.3g	0.2g
Carbohydrate of which sugars	19.4g 16.5g	15.5g 13.2g
Fat	0g	0g
Fibre	1.6g	1.3g
VITAMINS/ MINERALS	% RECOMMENDED DAILY AMOUNT	
Vitamin C	26%	
THIS PACK CONTAINS 4 SERVINGS		

INFORMATION

56 02025 / 020258
59   2

PURE-PAK™
OPEN OTHER SIDE

A colour control bar to check density of ink and other printing characteristics (see page 70-71).

Type needs to be bold and clean (preferably sans serif) on this form of packaging and at least 8pt size. Some examples of typefaces that pose problems are shown right.

Register and trim marks.

These packs (right) are printed by offset on standard packaging board and the design limitations of flexography and gravure do not apply.

Some of these packs use an uncoated board, which means that a coarser screen (120 or so) will have to be used.

AB

ABCD

ABC

Aa Bb

Aa Bb Cc

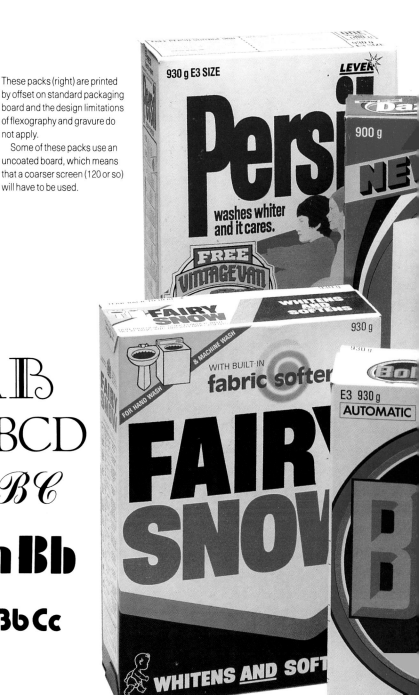

Some repro house nightmares

There are certain subjects or requests which are notoriously difficult and expensive for the repro house to achieve. Most repro houses will attempt to do them, but the cost will obviously reflect the amount of work involved and the sheer difficulty of achieving a good result.

Just a few are shown on this spread!

Moiré Moiré pattern (above) is unsightly but sometimes impossible to avoid, unless the designer can find a different subject.

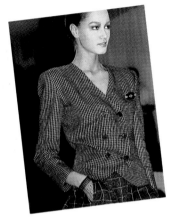

Gold lamé One of the trickiest of fabrics to repro (above). The gold, shiny quality of lamé is difficult to convey in a way that is true to the subject. Help your repro house by sending them a fabric swatch with the colour transparency.

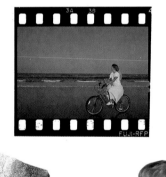

Hairline cut out Cutting out round a hairline (above) is difficult and time consuming, particularly if (as here) the hair tends to merge into the background, rather than being shot on a light background. The repro house will charge much more to do this than a straightforward cut out.

Bicycle cut out The same applies here (left), only more so. The sheer amount of work and time required to cut out between the spokes of the wheels is horrendous!

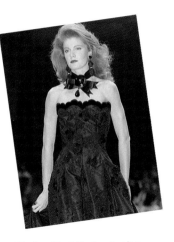

Black on black Black patterning on a black dress is very difficult to achieve, as the scanner really has nothing to pick up to give the required contrast (above). There is not a cost problem here, just the difficulty in giving the required result.

White detailing Retaining the brilliant whiteness of the dress, which is really paper white, while trying to hold the modelling of all the pleats and folds is difficult (below).

This modelling can only be created by dots of the four colours, and there is a danger that these will "dirty" the white. At best, the repro house can only achieve a compromise.

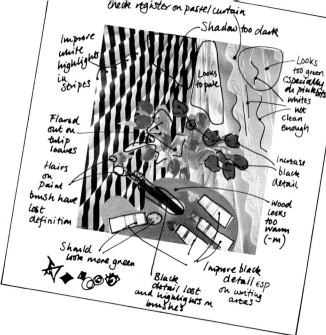

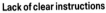

Lack of clear instructions Another nightmare for the repro house is when the designer has written an essay on every single subject, rather than giving concise, clear instructions (above) The repro house is left with the time-consuming task of reading all the comments and converting them into proper colour corrections.

Sending material in small batches A pet hate of repro houses (and probably designers) is breaking a job up into small batches . Every time a batch comes in, the repro house has to pick up the job again. When the batches are all at different stages, it is difficult to keep track of where material is, and batching can often mean "more haste, less speed".

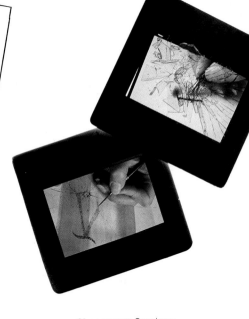

Glass mounts Opening a package of transparencies which have been left in their glass mounts, and which have broken in transit, is a repro house's nightmare: the splinters of glass will almost certainly have scratched the transparencies (above).

Ten golden rules

1 Specify tints in percentages, not Pantone colours.

2 Do not try to bluff if you lack technical knowledge. Admit it and ask for help.

3 The better the original, the better the proof.

4 Realize that the process cannot yield perfection. If a proof is very nearly right, do not correct.

5 Take care with fine type and reversals.

6 If additional work or a major correction is required, ask the repro house to quote before they do it.

7 Show the client and the repro house finished artwork to avoid costly corrections later.

8 When correcting proofs, say what you want, rather than tell the repro house how to do it.

9 Have the client sign off the final proof.

10 TALK to your repro house.

How do I check ozalids and film?

Normally, OZALIDS will be supplied by the printer rather than the repro house. This is because if the repro house has supplied page proofs completely made-up (see pages 56-57), there is no need for them to supply an ozalid. The page film simply goes to the printer, who imposes it, so that the pages fall in the correct place on the sheet to run in sequence. In theory, all the printer can do wrong is put the pages in the wrong order or out of position. With page film, the printer should not be able to alter anything within the page. However, it is worth checking the ozalid for scratches and damage as well as for position.

Where scatter proofs have been supplied by the repro house, the printer's ozalid needs much more careful checking, as the printer has done the page make-up and it is the first time the designer sees the type and pictures together.

To make an ozalid the printer will normally proof only the black and the most predominant of the colours (yellow, for example), which means that material which only appears in magenta or cyan will not show up. Here, the designer should point out what is missing and leave it to the printer to check the film.

Sometimes the repro house will supply an ozalid of a single page or picture, to show that a type correction, cropping or positional change has been made and a revised colour proof is not justified.

CHECKING FILM On most commercial or advertising jobs, the film can go straight from the repro house to the printer, without the designer seeing it, particularly with page film.

The need to check film occurs mainly in bookwork, where the pictures have been scatter proofed and the text film made elsewhere by the typesetter. Here, the designer will check the film for completeness and damage and compare it with the rough paste-up, so that when the printer starts imposition, everything has been checked on the film.

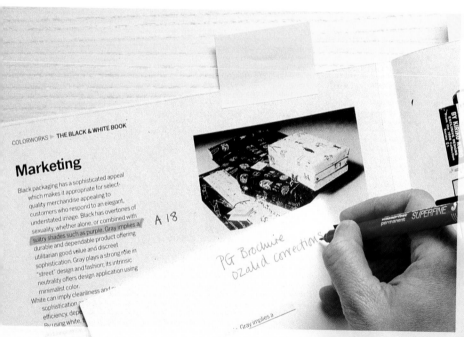

Correcting type In many cases if type is corrected at ozalid stage (to be avoided if possible), it will have to be reset and new camera-ready copy stripped in. In this instance, the typesetter should be asked to supply a "patch" of three or four lines, even if the correction affects only one line, to enable the repro house to position the corrected CRC more easily. Very minor type corrections can be done by the repro house. Examples are the deletion of a character. However, where the deletion requires respacing between words it is better to reset.

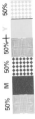

How do I check colour on press?

The vast majority of printing jobs are produced in the absence of the designer or client. However, where there is a long run of colour for a book or packaging, or where the colour is critical, the designer and/or client will be present, either for the first one or two sheets, or for the complete run.

This applies particularly to prestige promotional material, such as a corporate brochure or report and accounts. With such items, the designer should encourage the client to be present, and may have to insist on this. The reason is that sometimes compromises have to be made, for example with corporate colours (see pages 44-45). If the client is present, the problem and the need to compromise can be explained much more easily than after the event. If the client refuses to see such jobs on machine, it must be made clear that the designer assumes full authority to pass the job on the client's behalf without any financial penalty, should the job be criticized later.

Note that if the designer and/or client pass a job and the run is to the same standard as the sheet they have signed, the printer cannot be held responsible for any printing faults not picked up.

When making the press ready, the printer should have the marked colour proofs and progressives to refer to, as well as the marked ozalid proof. Before passing the colour, the designer should check the printed sheet against the ozalid, to ensure that any corrections have been carried out properly. Then the sheet should be checked for spots, which can sometimes occur in the platemaking process (unless they occur in the middle of a picture, they can usually be deleted from the plate, without removing it from the machine). Register should be checked to ensure that all the colour sets are positioned accurately.

Finally, the colour values should be checked. The colour can be adjusted by regulating the amount of ink released onto the inking rollers and then onto the plate. One major problem in adjusting colour on the machine is that it can only be done in tracks that is to say in strips parallel to the direction in which the sheets come off the machine. Therefore, if you increase the magenta in one picture, the magenta will be increased in all the other subjects in that track. Another problem occurs when the imposition dictates that the two halves of a double-page spread are in different tracks. Clearly, the two halves must match as closely as possible, without upsetting the colour balance of other subjects in the two tracks.

Decisions about colour adjustment need to be made quickly, either because the press is already running, or it is making ready and productive time is being lost. Checking colour on machine can be an intimidating experience until the designer has done it several times. However, the printer will usually advise and help the novice on how to achieve the best result.

Index

Credits

Quarto would like to thank the following for their help with this publication and for permission to reproduce copyright material. Special thanks must go to Art Directors Photo Library for all their help; and Peter Brehm of SWOP.

KEY: a = above, b = below, c = centre, r = right, l = left

33: The Face
38(ar)/**39**: Photographer Martin Norris
40/41: Art Directors Photo Library
44: Patricia Bayer/ Photographer, Eileen Tweedy
45: Rothmans UK Ltd
46/47: "Photo supplied courtesy of Du Pont Imaging Systems"
49: Art Directors Photo Library
50: Photographer Ian Sanderson
51: Reproduced courtesy of Aspen plc
52: (ar) Art Directors Photo Library
53: (br) Crosfield Electronics
57: Thanks to Image Bureau
58/59: Art Directors Photo Library
61: (bc) Collier Campbell

63: Art Directors Photo Library
64: E T Archive
65: (bl) Art Directors Photo Library
67: (1) © Du Pont reproduced with Du Pont's kind permission (2) © 1986 Graphic Arts Technical Foundation/GCA/ GATF Proof Comparator II (3) © 1989 Graphic Arts Technical Foundation/GATF 85-line Colour Control Bar (4) © Matchprint Color Element 3M (5) © 1981 System Brunner CH-6600 Locarno (6) © Kinmei, Japan
70/71: © 1981 System Brunner CH-6600 Locarno
72: (ar) Photographer Phil Starling
79: Art Directors Photo Library
80/81: Thomas Cook/Faraway Holidays
82: Photographer Phil Starling
83: E T Archive
84-87: Photographer Phil Starling
88-89: Photographer Martin Norris
100-101: Photographer Tony

McGee; Client Fiat (Auto) UK Ltd, The Yellowhammer Advertising Company Limited
102/103: Art Directors Photo Library
104/105: Art Directors Photo Library
110/111: Nick Clark
112/113: The Garden Picture Library
114/115: Pegasus Holidays (London) Limited
118/119: Photographer Tony Skinner; Client Fiat (Auto) UK Ltd, The Yellowhammer Advertising Company Limited
120/121: Art Directors Photo Library
122/123: Collier Campbell
126/127: Tag Heuer
133: Art Directors Photo Library
135: (b) Aesthedes Limited
138: (al) Niall McInerney, (ar) (bc) Art Directors Photo Library
139: (al) Niall McInerney

Every effort has been made to trace and acknowledge all copyright holders. Quarto would like to apologise if any omissions have been made.

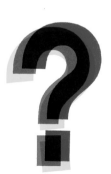